Your Child at Play:
Birth to One Year

Your Child at Play: Birth to One Year

Dr. Marilyn Segal

Newmarket Press
New York

To my five children, who gave me first-hand experiences with the joys of motherhood

Copyright © 1983, 1985 Marilyn Segal, Ph.D.
A Mailman Family Press book published by Newmarket Press, drawn from research conducted at Nova University, Ft. Lauderdale, Florida.
This book published simultaneously in the United States of America and in Canada.

3 4 5 6 7 8 9 0 F/C
   5 6 7 8 9 0 F/P

Library of Congress Cataloging in Publication Data

Segal, Marilyn M.
  Your child at play: birth to one year.

  Bibliography: p.
  1. Play. 2. Child development. 3. Infants.
I. Title.
HQ782.S425   1985   649'.5   85-325
ISBN 0-937858-50-1
ISBN 0-937858-51-X (pbk.)

The author gratefully acknowledges the continuing grant from the A. L. Mailman Family Foundation, Inc., which supported the writing of this book.

Volumes in the *Your Child at Play* series:
  Your Child at Play: Birth to One Year
  Your Child at Play: One to Two Years
  Your Child at Play: Two to Three Years
  Your Child at Play: Three to Five Years
Published simultaneously in hardcover and paperback editions

Manufactured in the United States of America

TABLE OF CONTENTS

Associate Authors:

WENDY MASI is a Developmental Psychologist and Associate Director of the Family Center at Nova University in charge of Family Programs. Dr. Masi served as an adjunct assistant professor at the University of Miami Medical School from 1976 through 1978 and developed an infant nursery training curriculum in conjunction with Dr. Tiffany Field. Dr. Masi lives in Ft. Lauderdale, Florida with her husband, Dr. Nicholas Masi, and her three children.

RONI COHEN LEIDERMAN received her B.S. from Boston University and her M.S. from Lesley College. She is the Assistant Director of the Family Center at Nova University and is a Ph.D. candidate in Applied Developmental Psychology. Ms. Leiderman resides in Ft. Lauderdale, Florida with her husband and two children.

CLAUDIA K. SOKOLOWSKI, M.Ed. has recently developed the curriculum and coordinated the Infant Awareness Program for Nova University. She has taught in the public schools of Florida and has worked with parents and children for the past eight years. She has taken an active interest in parent awareness and has conducted a variety of seminars for parents on infant stimulation. She is married and has two children that have participated in the programs.

INTRODUCTION

Some First Thoughts

For new parents and even experienced parents, the first year of a baby's life is full of wonderment and excitement. Changes take place at such a rapid rate that getting to know your baby is an almost daily challenge. When your baby is five or six months old you will look increduously at a newborn baby, "Was my baby ever that little?"

Your Child at Play: Birth to One Year is written for parents and caregivers who want to keep in close touch with their babies during the first twelve months. Organized on a month by month basis, it describes subtle developmental events so you can become better observers of your own baby's developments. At the same time it provides you with a wide selection of games and activities that you can enjoy with your baby.

Begin your reading of *Your Child at Play: Birth to One Year* by selecting the section that matches your child's developmental stage. (If your baby was premature or seems to be developing at a slow pace, select a chapter that is one or two months earlier than her chronological age.) Once you have found your starting point read the first section of the chapter. This section begins with Baby's Viewpoint, and presents a general overview of your baby's developmental status. The subsections that follow, Motor Skills, Seeing, Hearing and Feeling, and Knowing Your Baby, focus on the developmental changes that you can expect in the month ahead.

As you read through the first section don't expect that your baby will always follow the developmental course that we outline. Babies are quite different from each other and not ever completely predictable. For many babies development takes place at an uneven pace. At times your baby appears to be at a standstill. At other times baby will forge ahead at an astonishing pace. Babies also have different areas of strength or leading skills which serve as their cutting edge of development. For some babies this leading skill is physical, and the first indication of a developmental spurt is the achievement of a motor milestone. For other babies the developmental spurt may be marked by a new awareness of the properties of objects, or a new ability to communicate wants and needs.

The second section of each chapter is devoted to suggested activities. As you select the activities that you and your baby might enjoy keep in mind the following points.

1. Introduce playtime activities when your baby is happy and rested and don't be tempted to continue when your baby has had enough.
2. Be sensitive to your baby's cues. Babies have a way of letting you know when they are ready for a change.
3. Feel comfortable about changing activities to make them appropriate for you and your baby. The activities we describe are just suggestions. Use your own creativity and knowledge of your baby to improve on our ideas.
4. Recognize your baby's lead skill. Provide some activities that capitalize on your baby's developmental strengths and some activities that provide practice in areas where your baby is less advanced.
5. Remember that babies have their own threshold for stimulation. While some babies thrive on intense stimulation, other babies do better with a more subdued approach.
6. Make your baby a family affair. You will discover very soon that every member of your family has his or her own style of playing. It is good for your baby to experience these differences. And while every member of the family has something special to contribute to your baby, your baby gives something special to each member of the family.

An Apology

Like all authors we have been confronted with the problem of whether to use he, she or he/she when we mean either he or she. Because the he/she construction is awkward we have used the imperfect solution of alternating between he and she. On the even chapters we refer to the baby as "she"—on the odd chapters we use "he." Someday, we hope, a new combined he/she word will make its way into the dictionary.

THE NEWBORN
(BIRTH—ONE MONTH)

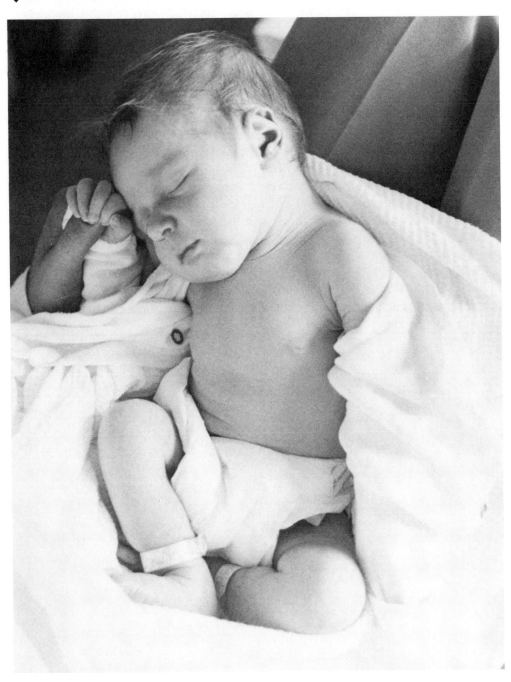

Baby's Viewpoint: Your newborn baby knows the world as a stream of fleeting sensations. All feelings, sounds, tastes and sights are new and unconnected. She has no sense of time, no awareness of space, no way of differentiating between "me" and "not me." Cause and effect have no place in your baby's scheme of things. Events happen because they happen. She feels a pang of hunger and hears her own cry. Did the cry come from inside her body or from somewhere outside? Did Mother's coming take away the cry and ease the pang of hunger? Your baby does not know the answer and cannot pose the question . . .

As crying follows distress and comforting follows crying your baby builds up a set of associations. She sees you beside her crib and anticipates feelings of comfort. Slowly over time and on an intuitive level she develops a sense of safety and security knowing that her needs will be met. As a parent you respond to your baby's growing trust, with increased confidence in yourself. You become aware of her leading skills, sensitive to her pace, and supportive of her needs. In every sense of the word you become the most reliable authority on the needs and personality of your baby.

During these first days and weeks of infancy you and your baby become intertwined in a love relationship. This ever strengthening bond is your baby's first lesson in loving. It is the prototype for other love relationships throughout your baby's life, and the source of energy for all she will ever learn.

Motor Skills

The newborn baby is unable to feed herself or move about, but she is far from helpless. She comes into the world with an impressive set of built-in reflex behaviors. For the most part these built-in reflexes are the key to the baby's survival. When we stroke a newborn baby's cheek, her head turns and she gropes for the nipple. When a nipple is placed in her mouth, she automatically swallows. Another set of reflexes protects a baby against physical harm. When the baby's nose and mouth are covered, she turns her head to the side. When an object moves in toward her face, she automatically blinks her eyes.

Some reflexes that are present in a newborn have no direct tie to survival but do provide information about the baby's developmental status. During a postnatal checkup the pediatrician may hold the baby in different positions, make a sudden loud sound, or pass his finger along the side of the baby's foot. As the baby reacts to these and other manipulations the pediatrician is assured that the newborn's reflexes are normal and her nervous system intact.

While most of the reflexes that are present in the newborn disappear during the first year of life, some reflexes serve as the basis of learned behavior. Sucking at first is a reflexive behavior, but as the baby gains experience she learns to alter her sucking technique according to what she is sucking. The same is true of the grasp reflex. A newborn baby will close her hand in the same way no matter what kind of object is placed in her palm. By the age of four months, her grasp will come under voluntary control. She will focus on an object and then reach out and grasp it.

Although we tend to think of all the new babies as starting from the same zero point, newborns are noticeably different in their level of motor development. Some new babies are remarkably inactive. Placed on their stomach or back they remain almost motionless until they are picked up and moved. Other babies are remarkably active. Placed face down in the crib they inch up to the top of the crib and wedge themselves in a corner. Some very active babies flip reflexively from stomach to back.

A second dimension of difference in new babies is their degree of muscle tone. Some babies appear to be especially tight, with knees pulled up, arms close to their bodies, and hands held tight in a fist. Other babies are more floppy, with less tone in their limbs.

A third difference among new babies is their level of sensory motor maturity. Some babies, especially babies who are small and/or premature, appear to be easily upset. A slight noise can jerk their whole being, and their arms and legs begin to flail in a kind of disorganized state. Sometimes, for no apparent reason a tremor travels through their bodies. Other babies appear to be quite well organized from the beginning. They have learned how to get their hands in or near their mouths and they use the hand-mouth position as a way of quieting down. When these babies kick their feet there is a rhythm and pattern to their movements.

The differences in activity level, muscle tone, and sensory motor maturity that we observe in newborns reflect differences in organization on a neurological level. Babies who are active, well-organized with good muscle tone are described by their parents as easy babies. Babies who are inactive, disorganized, and either flaccid or tight, are usually more difficult to take care of during the early months. Fortunately, with patience and loving care, most babies will overcome these immaturities and catch up with their peers.

Seeing, Hearing, and Feeling

Your baby enters the world with a built-in repertoire of adaptive skills. She blinks her eyes when a bright light is turned on or when an object comes toward her face. She tracks a moving target such as an approaching face for a short distance.

Your baby is also born with an innate capacity to use her senses to take in new information. Interestingly enough, she even shows visual preferences. She seeks out designs with a distinct center point, and is particularly attracted to moving objects and to black and white configurations. Think about the characteristics of human eyes. It's hard to escape the conclusion that the baby is uniquely programmed to make early eye contact with her parents.

In addition to innate visual skills, the newborn baby has remarkable auditory capabilities. Not only are we certain that a baby hears from the moment of birth, but there is strong evidence to suggest that the baby hears in the womb. The newborn will turn her head toward the source of sound, alert to a sound that is new, and tune out sounds that are repetitive, loud, or steady. Even more striking is the fact that the baby can discriminate between a human voice and any other sound. In other words, just as the baby is uniquely programmed to look into your eyes, she also has a built-in tendency to listen to your voice.

Although the newborn baby attends to sounds and turns toward the source of sound, her auditory and visual systems are not fully coordinated. When she hears a sound that is in front of her she does not automatically search with her eyes for the object that is making the sound. This kind of coordination takes time to develop. By giving the baby experiences with things that both look and sound interesting, parents lay the groundwork for the association of sight and sound.

We have talked so far about the baby's ability to see and hear. Let us talk about the other senses; taste, smell, and the sense of touch. Babies like things that are sweet, but reject food that is salty, sour, or bitter. They also turn away from smells that are strong and pungent.

We know too that new babies react to different tactile experiences. Brisk rubbing with a rough towel alerts a baby while a gentle massage can put a baby to sleep. Stroking your baby with the tip of your fingers or a soft, silky fabric can keep your baby quiet and alert. The feel of human skin holds a special attraction for a new baby. Nursing mothers often report that their baby sucks more contentedly when her hand is placed on their breasts.

Although we have described some of the typical ways in which new babies respond to different kinds of stimulation, the quality of a baby's response is different at different times. Dr. Prechtl, Dr. Brazelton and other students of the newborn describe the baby as having different states of arousal. These states of arousal are different ways of behaving. The sleeping baby may be in a deep sleep with slow even breathing and minimal movement, in irregular or REM sleep with eyes moving rapidly under her lids, or in a state of drowsiness. Awake, the baby may be in a quiet alert state, an active state, or a crying state.

The way the newborn responds to events in the environment is very much determined by her state of arousal. A baby who is in a quiet alert state may respond to the tinkle of a bell by a momentary cessation of activity followed by a visible effort to turn toward the source of sound. The same baby in an active or crying state may ignore the bell completely.

Knowing Your Baby

The newborn period is a time of adjustment for both the infant and her parents. Parents need to reorganize their daily routine in order to care for their baby. The baby must adjust both physiologically and psychologically to life outside the womb. An important part of the baby's adjustment is self regulation. The baby is learning to regulate her state of arousal so that she can move smoothly from a sleep state to a state of quiet alertness, or from an awake state to a state of quiet sleep. Much of your energy as a parent in these early weeks will be devoted to helping your baby make these transitions.

When a baby is in a state of quiet alertness she attends to sounds, stares at faces, and appears wide-eyed and aware. Because her energies are directed toward taking in information, parents have a special opportunity during this quiet state to stimulate and communicate with their infant. Too much stimulation, however, can be stressful. The newborn may not be able to look away when she is overwhelmed. It is important for parents to anticipate their baby's need for a rest. Pursing of the lips, tightened fists, or curling of the toes are all signs that baby needs a change of pace.

For most babies the state of quiet alertness follows a period of drowsiness. As you and your baby develop a daily routine you will instinctively find ways to help her achieve this state. Following feeding, for example, you may hold her over your shoulder in an upright position, or you may hold her in the crook of your arm and sway her gently back and forth.

A baby may sometimes reach a state of quiet alertness after a period of active crying. When an awake baby is fussy, it is natural for parents to try different techniques to keep the baby from crying. In some instances it is better to let the baby enter a crying state. The crying seems to relieve the baby's tension and allows her to reorganize her own behavior. Even if the baby has missed the state of quiet alertness on her way up from drowsiness to crying, she may achieve this quiet state on her way back down.

In general the most difficult state for a newborn to modulate without help is crying. Although babies differ in the amount of soothing they need and the kinds of soothing they respond to, all babies need help calming down.

Some babies quiet if they are held securely in their parents' arms or wrapped in a soft blanket. Other babies are upset by any kind of restraint and quiet more easily if they are placed on a flat surface with no covers or restraints. Most babies are comforted by movement, but the kind of movement that is most comforting is different for different babies. Which of the following kinds of movements work best with your baby?

Walking around the room with your baby held up to your shoulder.

Holding your baby over your shoulder, or against your shoulder, and rocking from side to side.

Holding your baby against your shoulder and patting her rhythmically on her back.

Holding your baby across your knees, moving your knees up and down or back and forth, or patting your baby gently on the buttocks.

Rocking very slowly in a rocking chair with baby prone across your knees or upright against your shoulder.

Fast, rhythmic rocking in a rocking chair.

Placing baby in a carriage and pushing it back and forth.

Taking your baby for a walk in a carriage, a backpack, or a front sling.

Placing your baby in a hammock and swinging it gently back and forth.

Taking your baby for a ride in the car.

Sounds as well as movements are soothing for a baby, but here again babies have their own preferences. Some babies quiet best to a steady sound, a clock ticking, a simulated heart beat, the whirr of a washing machine. Other babies react best to low-pitched talking, monotonous chanting, or quiet whispering. Still other babies prefer music: a lullabye, a music box, a classical record selection.

We have talked so far about how sensitive and loving parents help the infant make her first accomodations to life outside the womb. The baby influences her parents as well. She helps them adjust to their new role as parents. Within the first few weeks of life the young infant provides her parents with social cues and reinforcers that cement the parent-child bond.

The two major messages infants send are smiling and crying. Both follow a similar progression. In the first weeks they are spontaneous; that is, the baby is responding to internal physiological stimulation. Crying reflects internal discomfort or pain; smiling results from a sudden drop in the discharge level of the nervous system. Gradually the balance shifts. Crying and smiling are increasingly controlled by external events, and as a result the baby begins to communicate directly with her parents.

The development of the smile during the first month or two is particularly interesting. Initially fleeting smiles occur during sleep. Then by the second week the baby may smile with her eyes open, usually after feeding. This smile is accompanied by a kind of glassy, far away look. By the third or fourth week a qualitative change takes place. Baby attends to her parent's high-pitched voice, eye-to-eye contact is established, and the parent is rewarded with a truly social smile.

The baby who is happy and responsive most of the time inspires confidence in her parents, and gets the family off to a good start. The restless and irritable baby, the baby who is not easily soothed by the nurturant behaviors of her parents, presents a greater challenge. First-time parents are likely to interpret their baby's irritability as a sign of their own inadequacy. Once they recognize that the baby's fussiness is physiologically based, they regain their self-confidence and are able to manage these difficult first weeks. Through trial and error parents find special ways of quieting their baby—perhaps swaddling or vigorous rocking, or perhaps just allowing the baby to cry for a while until she falls asleep. Most important, they realize that their baby's difficulty with self-regulation does not indicate a long term personality characteristic.

During their first month with a newborn baby most parents will experience some negative emotion. The young mother, perhaps suffering from postpartum blues—or perhaps exhausted as a result of the delivery and subsequent sleepless nights—may find herself sliding into a mysterious depression, or getting snappish or unduly angry with other members of the family. The father, despite his proud smile, may sometimes feel that the baby is taking away not only a portion of his freedom, but also a portion of his wife's concern. As babies get older, they tend to sleep longer, and parents learn to adjust to a different sleep schedule. As the family adjusts to the presence of one more member these first tensions disappear, and the stage is set for a mutually rewarding relationship between parents and baby.

SUGGESTED ACTIVITIES FOR THE NEWBORN

An Introduction

The most important task that your baby has to accomplish in the first month is adjustment to life outside the womb. Much of the time your baby will be asleep. During her waking hours, she will be tuned into her physiological needs. Periods of quiet alertness, when your baby is ready to take in new information, are sparse and short lived. This means that you should not plan on a special play period for a newborn baby. Simply take advantage of spontaneous opportunities. These opportunities are most likely to arise when your baby is fed and contented. Remember that babies have different thresholds for stimulation, and if you overstimulate your baby you may change her state from quiet alertness to fussiness or crying.

Setting the Stage

Handle Baby Just Enough

Your baby needs and loves to be handled. Judge how much holding your baby enjoys. Some babies get tense and irritable from too much handling. A fussy baby may calm when carried in an infant "snugli" carrier. Too little handling, on the other hand, can leave the baby listless and unresponsive.

Change Baby's Position

Place the baby in different positions when she is awake. Sometimes she can be on her stomach, sometimes on her back, sometimes on her side. Your baby will practice moving her arms and legs in different positions.

Baby Calendar

Hang a calendar with a pencil near baby's changing table or dresser. New accomplishments and progress can be recorded in each space.

Have a Good Time With Baby

Smile and laugh with your baby. A baby seems to be able to tell when you are having fun with her.

**Don't
Worry
About
Spoiling**

Respond quickly to your baby's needs. If you give a baby appropriate attention when she needs it, she will not ask for attention when she doesn't need it.

**Play It
Safe**

Take your baby home from the hospital in a safety approved car seat.

Playtime

Seeing:

**Suspend a
Musical Mobile
Over Baby's
Crib**

During moments when your baby is quiet and awake she will catch sight of the mobile and her eyes will follow its movements. This will awaken her interest in the world outside of her crib. Musical mobiles are especially attractive to young infants.

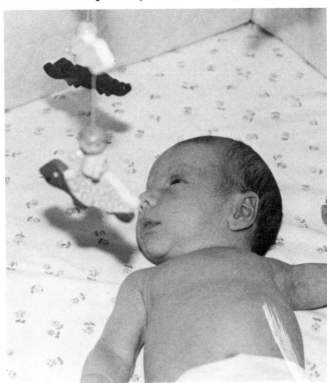

**Move a
Flashlight
Back and Forth**

Cover a flashlight with red or yellow cellophane. While your baby is on her back, move the light slowly from side to side. At first your baby will look at it just for a second, but after a while she will follow it with her eyes.

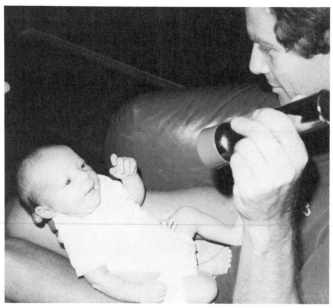

**Stick Out Your
Tongue!**

Some 2–3 week olds can imitate you when you stick out your tongue. Give it a try!

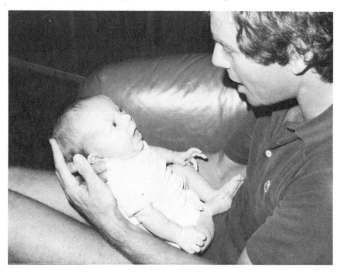

Listening:

Hang Up a Japanese Woodchime

Hang a Japanese woodchime in a place where baby can watch it move and listen to the sound. This will give your baby an opportunity to associate a pleasant sight with a pleasant sound. If the chime is over the crib your baby is likely to watch it for a few minutes and then drop off to sleep.

Dance to the Music

Your newborn will enjoy the familiar rocking movements she has felt for so many months. Listen to music as you hold and gently dance with your baby.

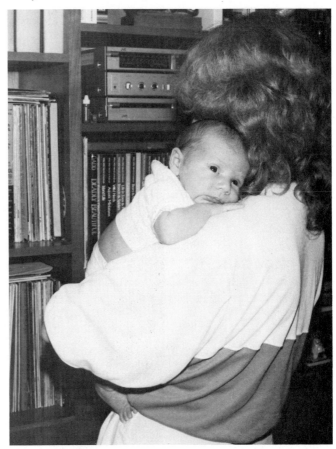

**Shake a Rattle
Near Baby**

Shake a rattle first on one side of the baby's head, then on the other. Begin by shaking it slowly—then vigorously. After awhile, your baby will realize that the sound she hears comes from somewhere outside herself. She will search with her eyes for the thing that is making the sound. (An aluminum juice can half filled with beans makes an excellent rattle).

Feeling:

**Place a Finger
or Rattle in
Baby's Palm**

Place your own finger or a rattle in the palm of your baby's hand. Your baby will tighten her fingers around it.

Exercising:

Kicking Practice

Place your baby on a firm mat (a crib mattress or playpen mat is fine) without any covers. Give your baby a few minutes to kick her feet and move her arms. If she begins to cry, try to calm her by gently rocking.

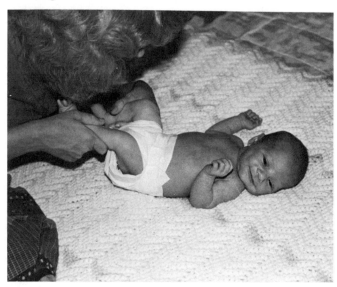

Daily Routines

Mealtime:

Keeping Mealtime Happy

Whether you breastfeed or bottle feed your baby, feeding time should be happy and relaxing for both baby and you. And remember, your baby knows better than you when she has had enough to eat so don't push her to have a little more. Tension is catching and so is confidence.

Reach Out and Touch

As your baby is feeding, gently massage her head, fingers and shoulders. Your baby will associate her feeding with your loving touch. Some babies enjoy listening to singing while they suck. Other babies will listen to their mother's voice and forget to suck. If your baby is easily distracted, reserve your singing for burp time or pause time.

Bathtime:

Beginning Bath

Bathe your baby in a baby bathtub. (Check with your doctor before giving your baby her first bath). Talk or sing softly as you wash your baby, rubbing gently with a soft washcloth. Place a towel in the bottom if baby is squirmy and needs a softer cushion.

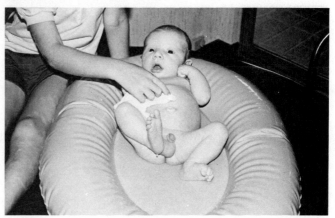

**Communicating
Through Touch**

After her bath, your baby is ready to be massaged. Using baby oil or a cold pressed vegetarian oil gently massage her arms, hands, legs, feet, back, tummy and buttocks. Continue only as long as your baby is quiet and content.

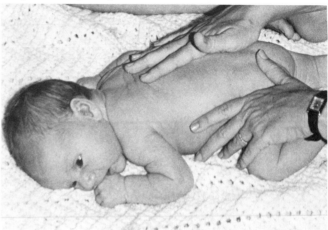

Diapering/
Dressing:

Tummy Kisses

As you change your baby's diapers, gently kiss tummy, toes and fingers. This gentle stimulation helps baby develop an early awareness of her body parts. Not only is baby becoming aware of herself but she is also feeling your expression of love.

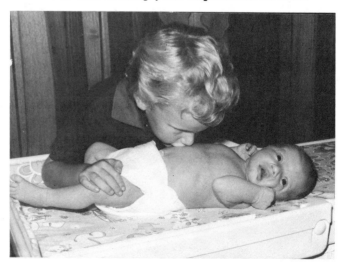

Dressing Down

Don't overdress your baby. If your room is between 68° and 75°, your baby will be quite comfortable in a shirt and diaper. Babies get hot, "rashy," and uncomfortable when they are overdressed.

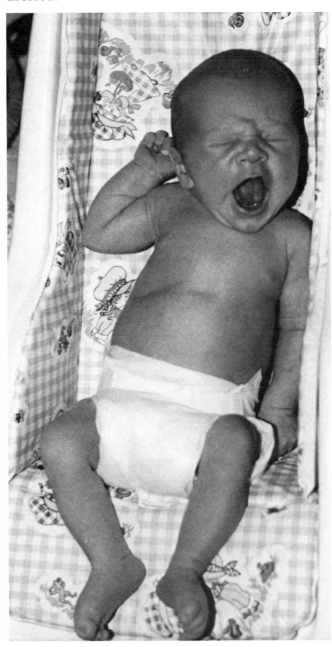

Quiet Time:

Play a Radio for Baby

Play a radio or wind up a music box when you place baby in her crib. Quiet music helps to soothe your baby.

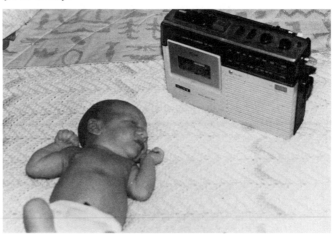

Tape Record Your Washing Machine

As an alternative to the expensive Teddy Bear toy with taped sounds of the uterus, try taping your dishwasher or washing machine. The whooshing sounds played back for your baby help to soothe and comfort her.

Give Baby a Musical Toy

By associating a soft musical toy with sleeptime from a very early age you can create an early attachment to a "huggee." This "huggee" will continue to help your baby fall asleep in later months when some babies resist being placed in a crib.

Use a Pacifier

Put a pacifier in baby's mouth on her way to sleep. Babies who learn to use pacifiers at an early age are able to "self-comfort" on the way to sleep. If your baby resists a pacifier at first you may have to hold it in her mouth for a few seconds until she gets used to it. If she is still resistant, try a different kind.

Take Your Baby on a Carriage Walk

Weather permitting, take your baby for a carriage ride. The steady movement will help your baby fall asleep.

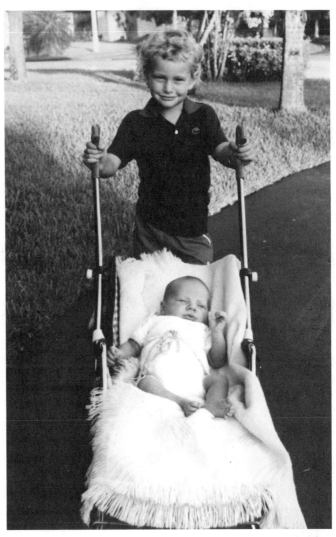

Shadow Play

Baby wakes frequently during the night. Leaving a soft light on enables your baby to explore the shadows of her immediate surroundings.

Swaddling and Plump Pillows

Your newborn has been sleeping in very tight quarters for the past few months. She may enjoy being swaddled in a baby blanket or sleeping with pillows propped up around her. Hammocks that fit inside a regular crib can be purchased in many stores. An added feature in some of these hammocks is a simulated heart beat. The steady rhythm reminiscent of the sounds in the womb calms and quiets baby.

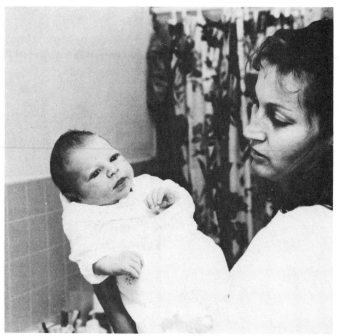

ONE MONTH

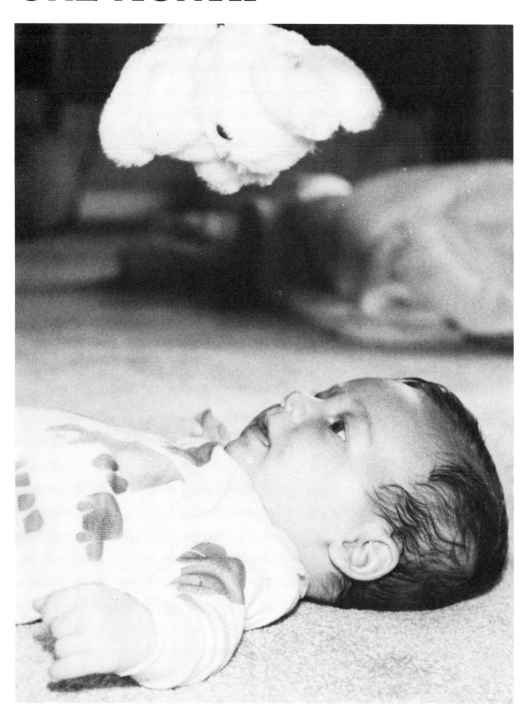

Baby's Viewpoint: In the newborn chapter we talked about the beginning of a communication system between parent and child. During the second month of life we will see this system developing as the baby becomes increasingly responsive to parent-child exchanges. At the same time we will see the baby developing greater muscle control and an expanded capacity to respond to the sights and sounds he experiences.

As a baby increases his capacity to take in and respond to new information, parents become more aware of their baby's personality. Already at one month old, you can identify characteristics of your baby that set him apart from other same age babies. In face to face conversations you become attuned to your baby's natural rhythm, and you recognize when to provide more stimulation and when to turn away. You learn new ways of handling your baby during bouts of irritability. You discover techniques to help him maintain a state of quiet alertness, or settle down to sleep.

One of the ways that you can help your baby become better organized is to teach him how to suck a pacifier. Some babies suck a pacifier automatically, but others will reject it forcefully. If your baby resists or spits out a pacifier, be persistent. Hold the pacifier in your baby's mouth while you rock him and sing to him. Buy two or three different kinds of pacifiers so that you can discover the one that is easiest for him to suck. After a while your efforts will pay off and your baby will use the pacifier as a way of calming himself down and putting himself to sleep. The pacifier is a tool that both you and your baby will appreciate in the months ahead.

Motor Skills

The one month old is gaining control of his body. He has lost some of the jerky, spasmodic movements, and is beginning to move his arms and legs in a smooth and rhythmic pattern. The tremors and startles that are so characteristic of the newborn are beginning to disappear.

One of the most noticeable changes is the baby's increase in head control. When placed on his stomach in the crib, the baby can move his head effortlessly from side to side. Especially strong babies may even lift their head off the sheet and look around the crib. This increased head control is also evident when baby is held on your shoulder. However, no matter how strong your baby is, head control is far from perfect. Make sure to "cradle" his head in your arms when you lift him out of the crib or carry him around the room.

Although month old babies do not usually move around, occasionally we will find an active month old who will "wiggle" up to a corner of his crib or even turn from stomach to back. But even inactive babies may be capable of sudden movement. To be on the safe side, it's better not to leave even the tiniest baby by himself on a high place.

In addition to an improvement in head control, the one month old baby has become much more adept at waving his arms and kicking his legs. Not only can he exercise his arms and legs in a smooth and rhythmic pattern, but he can speed up or slow down his movement in rhythm with a human voice. When you speak to your baby in a slow and steady rhythm his arm and leg movements are slow and steady. Try speaking faster and with more excitement and watch how his kicking speeds up.

Seeing, Hearing, and Feeling

When we talked about the newborn baby we talked about states of arousal. We said that babies have different ways of being in the world, different ways of being asleep, and different ways of being awake. In the month old baby these states are more discrete. It is easy to tell when your baby is in a quiet or an active sleep, and when baby is in a quiet alert state rather than an awake and active state.

In the quiet alert state a one month old baby can follow a moving object with his eyes. He focuses with interest on an object or a picture that is eight to twelve inches in front of him. If the object is especially interesting the baby might even "coo" at it. Then after a few minutes the baby looks away. This is called "habituation." It is as if he is saying, "Yes, I know that object now." If you change the object that is in front of the baby, or introduce a second object, his visual exploration begins again.

The one month old baby is interested in new sounds as well as new sights. He can tell the difference between talking and other sounds, and shows a definite preference for listening to a voice. When first presented with a new sound the baby "alerts," that is, he stops moving his arms and legs and appears to be listening to the sound. After two or three presentations of the same sound, the baby habituates and does not attend to the sound. If you change the sound, such as changing from a bell to a squeak toy or a rattle, the baby will attend to the new presentation.

At one month old, baby is getting better at associating the things he hears and the things he sees. With a little practice he will be able to look up at his bell as soon as he hears its tinkle. Baby reacts differently to different kinds of sounds. Music quiets him, a loud noise startles him, a high pitched whistle or an interesting jingle will hold his attention.

Knowing Your Baby

From the moment of birth babies are distinct individuals, differing from one another in many important ways. By the time baby is one month old parents begin to really know him. They can describe their baby on a continuum from quiet to restless, from contented to irritable, from active to slow moving, from easy to soothe to difficult to soothe, from predictable to erratic, from quick to respond to slow to respond. They know how their baby likes to be held, the position that works best for putting him to sleep. They can identify his pain cry, his hunger cry, and the cry that means "There is nothing really wrong. I just want some cuddling."

The one month old baby has lost his sleepy newborn look. He stays awake for longer periods of time before and after feedings, but he still is not ready for too much stimulation. When the baby is exposed to too much noise, too much light, or too much jostling around, he cannot sort out all of the separate sensations. Overwhelmed by it all, he reacts with irritability. In fact, many one month olds have a particular period during the day when they are prone to become overtired and fussy. During this period of restlessness, some babies respond to cuddling, rocking, or rhythmic pattings on the backside. Others will stop their crying and go to sleep if they are wrapped in a blanket or tucked snuggly in a bassinet.

A very active or restless baby, however, may not respond to any of these techniques, and his high-pitched insistent crying creates tensions in the household. This hard to soothe baby may need to release built-up tensions in a short period of crying. The following procedure works well for parents with a hard to soothe baby.

1. Complete bedtime routines such as feeding, diapering, bathing, and massaging at a relaxed and steady pace.

2. Sit in a rocking chair in a semi-darkened room. Hold your baby over your shoulder while you rock gently back and forth singing a tune. (If your baby tenses up in the over-the-shoulder position place him on his stomach across your knees or put him in a large comfortable carriage that can be shaken gently). Chant to your baby in a low, steady voice.

3. After five minutes of rocking, listen to the sound of his cry. Is he beginning to settle down? Is the cry less piercing and intense? If you feel that the cry is beginning to sound sleepier and less urgent continue to rock for another five minutes.

4. Perhaps your baby's cry has maintained or regained its frantic quality. In this case, place your baby gently on his stomach in the crib. Turn on a soft radio or music box and tip toe out of the room.

5. If the crying continues for longer than ten minutes, go through the routine again. Make sure that your pace is consistent, calm, quiet and self-assured.

6. Finally, if your baby continues to have problems settling down check with your pediatrician.

Although a baby at one month is not ready to face a crowd, he does enjoy social interaction. Baby can begin a "face to face" game with his parents. Parent and baby look at each other, look away, then meet with their eyes again. In this familiar routine, parent and baby are practicing a kind of turn taking routine which is the beginning step in language learning. After a while baby begins to make cooing noises as a part of this conversation. Although his repertoire of sounds may be limited to one or two front vowel sounds, in a very real sense he is learning how to converse.

It is fun to watch a parent engaging in a conversation with his month old baby. He may raise his eyebrows, open his eyes wide, and round his mouth.

Or he may knit his brow, squint his eyes and purse his lips. His head may nod and move in closer to the baby's face, or his head may be withdrawn slightly and turned to the side. During these unconscious antics the parent is modeling for the baby, in an exaggerated way, the non-verbal components of our language system. An open expression, with face fully presented, signals a desire to interact. It is an invitation to the baby to respond. A more closed expression, with face averted, signals a temporary pause in the conversation. The parent is acknowledging that the baby is momentarily uncomfortable and wants a short break.

These early conversations, as brief as they are, follow a predictable course. At first the parent's voice is high pitched in order to capture the baby's attention. As baby responds with ah's and oh's the parent becomes more animated and baby reaches a crescendo of excitement. As the baby's excitement subsides, the parent's voice lowers and parent looks away. In a few seconds parent and baby face each other again and a new exchange begins. As parent and baby practice these back and forth conversations, a smooth routine is established that both baby and parent enjoy.

SUGGESTED ACTIVITIES

Setting the Stage

Baby Talk

A baby's favorite sound is a human voice. Greet your baby as you come into the room and talk to your baby whenever you are together. Use a high pitched voice when you want to get your baby's attention, and a low-pitched voice when you want to soothe your baby. Changing from high pitch to lower pitch and back again to high pitch is a way of maintaining attention.

Father Play

Father play is different from mother play. Because each parent brings his baby a different kind of stimulation it is important for parents to share the routine care of babies.

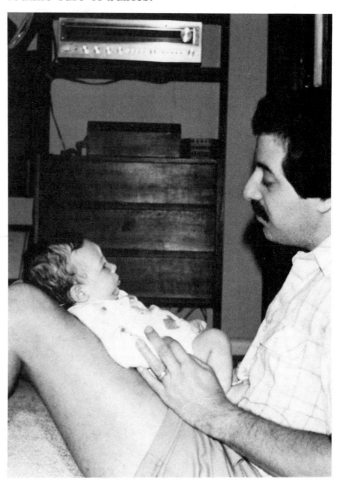

Change Your Baby's Outlook

Place your baby in different positions so that he can look at different things. When taking your baby on an automobile ride, for example, place a bright pattern over the car seat to make his view exciting. (Make sure your baby is in a safety-approved car seat whenever you are in the car).

Playtime (Seeing, Listening, Feeling, Exercising)

Seeing:

Move a "Plate Puppet" In and Out

Make a simple plate puppet by drawing a face on a paper plate and pasting on a tagboard handle. Move the plate puppet in and out and back and forth about ten inches from your baby's eyes. After awhile the baby will not only follow the plate puppet with his eyes, but will greet it with a smile.

Tracking Fun

Let baby follow a rattle, a flashlight, or a brightly colored toy with his eyes. With the object 10–12 inches away from baby, move the object from left to right. When baby can follow it across the midline, introduce up and down tracking from baby's hairline to his chin. Finally, experiment with a circular movement. Remember to be sensitive to your baby and stop playing when he has had enough or seems frustrated.

Look at Me

Let baby track your face. As you move from left to right, baby will follow you with his eyes and turn his head.

Bouncing Pet

Attach a piece of elastic to a small stuffed animal. Attach the elastic to the ceiling. Position baby under it and make the animal jump and bounce. In later months, baby will try to catch and grasp it.

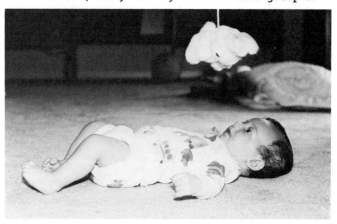

See-Through Crib Bumpers

Using clear plastic crib bumpers lets your baby see outside the crib.

Let Baby Watch a Mobile

Hang a mobile over baby's crib. As you select a mobile, think of how the mobile looks from the baby's point of view. Place it on one side for a few days and then change it to the other side. When you feel that your baby can focus on the mobile for a few moments, place a mobile on each side of the crib. After a while your baby will shift his gaze from one mobile to the other.

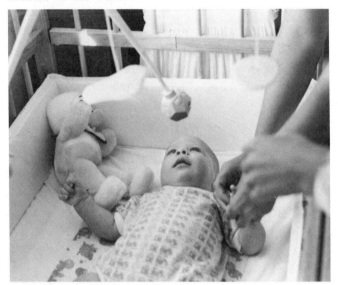

Listening:

Nursery Rhyme Time

Introduce your baby to the rhythm and cadence of a nursery rhyme. Use old favorites like "Rock-A-Bye-Baby," "One, Two, Buckle My Shoe," and "Where is Thumbkin?" or make up your own. Take a familiar tune and simply change the words. This jingle goes to "Frère Jacque:"

Hello Baby, Hello Baby,
How are you? How are You?
Oh! I love you so much,
Oh! I love you so much,
Yes I do. . . . .
Yes I do.

Jingle Bell Booties

Tie a bell onto each of baby's booties. Each time he kicks he will be rewarded with a jingling sound.

Where Am I

Talk to baby from different places in the room. As he searches with his eyes for you, he is beginning to coordinate sight and sound.

Feeling:

Rub Baby's Fingers and Toes

Rub fingers and toes one at a time. Baby will enjoy the sensation and increase his body awareness.

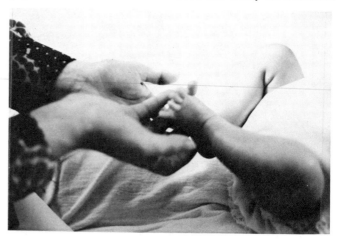

Let Baby Feel Different Fabrics

Rub the baby's arms and legs with different textured feel mittens—silk, velvet, satin, wool, flannel, or terry cloth.

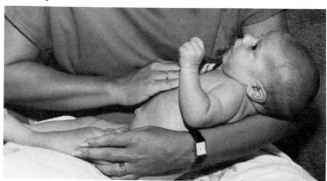

Light Touch

Stroke your baby gently with a paint brush, a feather, or a cotton ball. He will enjoy the sensation.

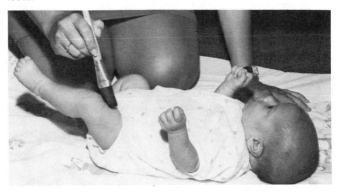

Smells—Cotton Ball Sniff

Dip cotton balls into different fragrances such as cologne, mint, and vanilla. Your baby will develop his sense of smell.

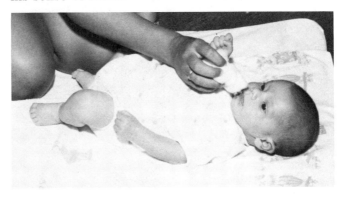

Exercising:

Move Baby's Arms Up and Down

With baby lying on his back, lift his arms gently up and down over his head, and then in and out. Chant a song at the same time:

Up-up-up little one.
Stretching, stretching is such fun.
In and out, let us go.
Not too fast and not too slow.

Bicycle Fun

Lie baby on his back and gently move his legs in a bicycle movement. Try singing a song like "The Wheels On The Bus Go Round and Around" as you exercise together.

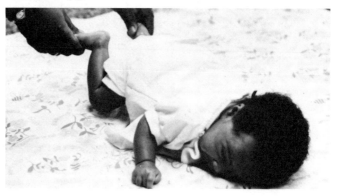

Looking Up

Put baby on his tummy on the floor. Get down on the floor with him and show baby a bright toy as you call his name. This encourages baby to lift his head and exercise his neck, back and arm muscles.

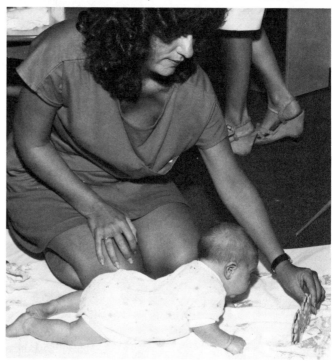

Looking Up at Mommy

Try the same activity again but this time you lie on your back and put your baby on your tummy. Call to your baby and encourage him to lift his head to see you.

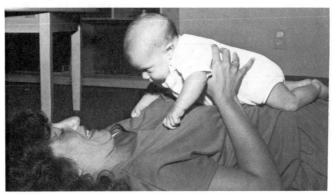

Daily Routines

Mealtime:

Change Positions

Breast fed babies naturally change positions while nursing. If your baby is bottle fed, alternate sides so baby can see things from a different perspective.

Cover Baby's Bottle

If your baby is not breast feeding, slip a cover over his bottle and let him feel the bottle as he sucks. Bottle covers can be bought in stores, but a tennis sock works just as well.

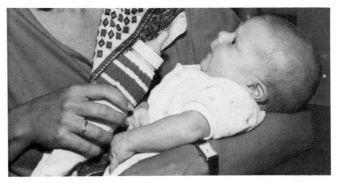

Use a Bright Towel at Feeding

Place a brightly colored towel over your shoulder while feeding the baby, or wear a bright scarf. Your baby will enjoy looking sometimes at your face, and sometimes at the towel. If your baby is distracted by the towel, you may not want to use it until feeding is over.

Bathtime:

Loving Touch

Continue massaging your infant. Select a favorite lullabye to sing during the massage. Your singing and your touching will combine to make your baby feel relaxed and secure.

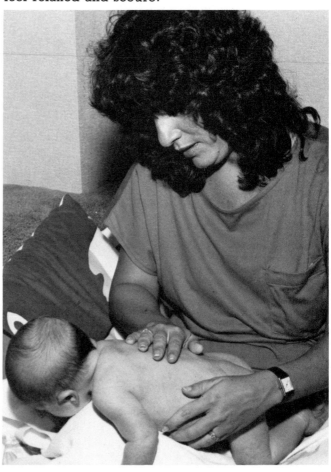

Wrap Up Baby
After baby's bath, use his towel to play a game of "peek-a-boo."

Diaper Time:

Diversion
Hang some lightweight toys over baby's changing table. Baby will stay still for a moment as he rediscovers each toy.

Blow on Baby's Arms and Tummy
Blow warm breath on arms and tummy. As the baby focuses attention on different parts of his body he learns more about himself.

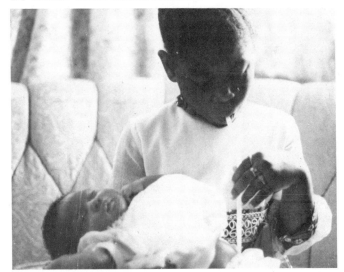

Quiet Time:

Fluttering Ribbons
Attach short lengths of colored ribbons to a plastic ring. Hang the ring near the baby. Open a window or turn on an electric fan to set the ribbons in motion. Baby will enjoy watching the movement on his way to sleep.

Rest Awhile

Let baby rest on your chest. Your rhythmic breathing and voice vibrations are soothing and comforting for baby. You'll both enjoy the closeness.

TWO MONTHS

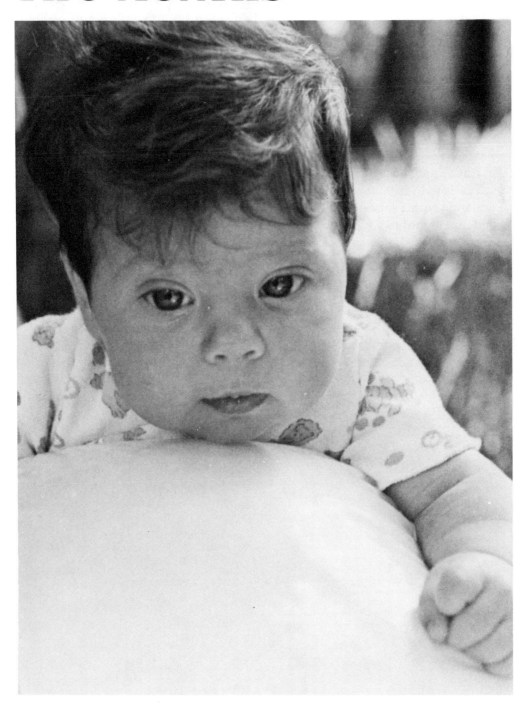

Baby's Viewpoint: Compared to the newborn the two month old is quite sophisticated. She is no longer a slave to built-in reflexes. After two months of practice she has modified these built-in reflexes to serve her own purposes. Rather than reacting in an automatic way to visual, auditory and tactile sensations, she uses new information to modify her behavior.

At two months old your baby spends most of her waking hours attending to outside stimulation. She is interested in listening for noises and scanning the room for new sights. A novel sight seems to give her pleasure which she expresses by a fixed look. Baby gets special pleasure out of watching her own hand, and is beginning to master the technique of keeping her hands in view.

The face to face conversations described in the one month section continue but with a subtle change. Although you are still the one who initiates and maintains the exchange, your baby has learned how to signal a pause. She alternates between looking at you and turning away, and in this way she is able to keep "conversing" for a longer time without getting overloaded.

Another important change at two months old is the frequency of smiling. At three weeks a baby is most likely to smile at the sound of a familiar voice. At four weeks a baby is most likely to smile at a familiar face. Now at two months your baby smiles not only at faces but at interesting sights and sounds and is not so likely to be turned off by intense stimulation.

Motor Skills

Although no major motor milestones are achieved between one month and two months, there is a significant qualitative change in the way your baby moves her body. Whether she is at rest or at play, random uncoordinated movements are few and far between, and the movements that we do see appear to be in the baby's control. Put to the breast for nursing, a baby no longer depends on reflex behavior to guide her to the nipple. After a few adjustments of head and neck she grasps the nipple with her lips and immediately starts to suck.

Baby's improved sucking ability is not only apparent during nursing. In between feedings, a two month old baby will suck at almost anything that is placed in her mouth, her own hand, a pacifier, the corner of a blanket, or, Mother's finger. She knows the difference, however, between sucking for exercise and sucking to satisfy hunger. When she is not hungry she will suck contentedly on the pacifier. When she is ready for nursing, she spits out the pacifier and cries.

Another sucking achievement of many two month old babies is purposeful and coordinated thumb sucking. At a younger age your baby sucked her thumb if it happened to land in her mouth. When the thumb fell out she cried. Now, at two months old your baby succeeds in getting both the hand and mouth under her control.

Because your baby still has a strong grasp reflex, it is easy to place a rattle into your baby's hand. Your baby may show her interest in the rattle by shaking the hand that is doing the holding. We may even see a baby bring the rattle to her mouth. She probably views the rattle as an extension of her hand, however, and not as an object to be sucked, for when the rattle drops from her hand she shows no sign of being perturbed.

In addition to improved hand and sucking skill, the two month old shows a definite improvement in head control. By now, most babies will lift their heads up when lying on their stomach and can hold their head upright for a few seconds when they are held in a standing position. An especially strong baby may be able to support herself on her arms when she is lying on her stomach.

Arms and legs are more active now. Your baby's arms are extended above her head in play. Her head and body twist from side to side. She moves her arms and legs up and down in a kind of rhythmic motion. Some babies, when lying on their stomachs, will begin to make crawling movements with their knees, using first one knee and then the other.

Seeing, Hearing, and Feeling

A clear example of the ability to modify behavior in response to new information is the baby's achievement of eye-hand coordination. At first, your baby examines her hand much as she would a new mobile—looking it up and down, inspecting the finger, the thumb, the sleeve of her nightgown. Gradually she discovers that she can increase the fun of hand-watching by moving her hand around. By the end of the second month she may open and close her fingers, focusing her whole attention on watching a hand in action. It seems that she is aware that the hand she is looking at belongs to her, and that she can make it perform.

The two month old also is able to follow an object visually when it is several feet away. She is particularly adept at this if the "object" she is watching is swinging or fluttering, or if it happens to be an older sister or brother. Most babies, by the end of the second month, have established a clear connection between seeing and hearing in a familiar situation. They may associate a pleasant sound with a bell and, when they hear the tinkling, they turn to look for its source.

Hearing, like vision, becomes more sophisticated in the third month. Baby becomes attentive to sounds, even soft ones—the telephone ring, the window shade flopping, the sound of Mommy's footsteps. As she did at an earlier age, the baby tends to freeze when first noticing an interesting sound. Her legs stop kicking, and her arms stop waving. Then, as the baby sees the source of the sound, she resumes the active movement of arms and legs.

Finally, your baby has more opportunity to learn how things feel because she keeps her hands open most of the time. She seems already to notice the difference between hard and soft, and enjoys the feeling of something soft placed in her hand. As baby continues to explore these tactile sensations, she stores up new information about the outside world.

Knowing Your Baby

By the third month, baby has mastered the art of smiling, and will smile at anyone who bends over the crib. In fact, she smiles at anything that looks like a face. A Pinocchio puppet, a witch's mask, a plate with two eyes, will be greeted with the same smiling response. At about the same time baby learns to smile, she begins to make talking sounds. This developmental state is the beginning of babbling. Baby will start by saying ah-ah-ee-ee or eh-eh as a sort of experiment, and then repeat the string of sounds over and over again. She seems to be intrigued with the sounds she is producing, and will often stay contentedly in her crib listening to her own sounds.

When an adult joins the vocal play, the baby is delighted. The adult imitates the baby's sounds, the baby coos back, and a kind of "conversation" begins. In addition, parents appear to enjoy mirroring the facial expressions of their two month olds. If baby opens up her mouth, Mother opens up her mouth. If baby squints her eyes, Mother squints her eyes. This behavior provides the baby with feedback that helps her learn about herself.

Baby now needs adults for more than food and comfort. A propped up bottle is no substitute for a talking, laughing, singing, touching parent. Baby needs people to play with her and to respond to what she does. Parents who find time to talk with, smile with, and coo back to baby during each of her waking periods are helping their baby develop important social skills.

SUGGESTED ACTIVITIES

Setting the Stage

Don't Overdress Your Baby

When the baby begins an activity period, make sure that her clothing is loose—the less she wears—the better. Remember that a baby is more active when she is a little cool.

Put Baby in a Baby Bounce Chair

Make sure that your baby has something interesting to look at during her waking hours. Change your baby's perspective by sitting her in an infant seat or in a baby bounce chair.

Listen to Baby Then Respond

Imitate the sounds your baby makes. Listen for her to repeat the sound, then imitate it again. Make sure to look in the baby's eyes during these conversations.

**Sing as You
Take Care
of Baby**

Learn some little jingles to go along with different activities such as bathing, feeding, and exercising. (To Twinkle Twinkle Little Star):

Splash splash splash, my little fish
Make a big splash if you wish.
Splash the water all around.
Listen to the splashing sound.

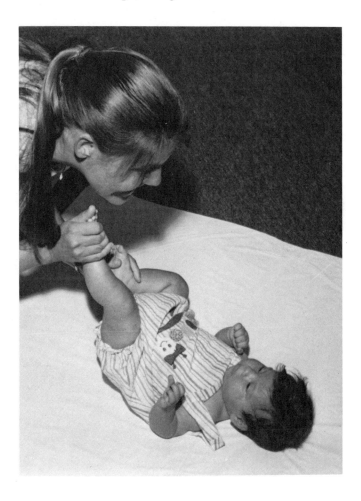

Sibling Fun

Give baby time to be with his older sisters and brothers. Their attention will entertain and stimulate baby.

Camera Ready!

Remember to keep a loaded camera handy. A photo album is your best way to record the day-by-day changes and recapture the happy moments.

Take Baby Along

Your baby will enjoy accompanying you as you make visits to stores and friends. The new sights, sounds and smells serve to stimulate your baby.

Playtime

Seeing:

Let Baby Wear a Wrist Band or Brightly Colored Socks

Make your baby a pair of wrist bands or buy a pair of brightly colored infant socks. Sometimes put the band or sock on the right hand, sometimes on the left and sometimes on both. As your baby moves her hands around in front of her eyes, she will discover how to manage her hands so that they stay where her eyes can watch them.

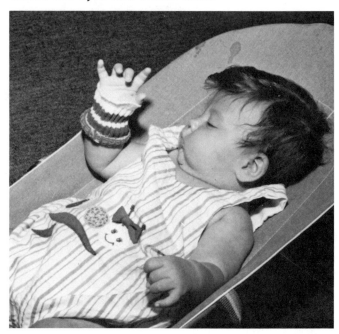

**Let Baby Watch
a Hand Puppet**

Move the hand puppet up and down, back and forth, and around in a circle within the baby's line of vision. Giving your baby practice in tracking develops her visual skills.

**Let Baby Hold a
Squeak Toy**

Put a squeak toy in your baby's hand. The accidental squeak will help her become aware of what her hand is doing.

**Let Baby Watch
a Finger Puppet**

Put a puppet on your finger and let the baby watch it dance. The sillier looking the puppet, the more the baby seems to enjoy it.

**Show Baby a
Reversible
Plate Puppet**

Make a reversible puppet out of a paper plate and a stick. Put a happy face on one side and a sad face on the other side. Move the plate puppet back and forth in front of baby. Show her the sad side and then the happy side. You will find that the baby loves to look at a face, and will soon begin to talk to it. The fact that the face keeps changing keeps up the baby's interest.

**String Up a
Convertible
Cradle Gym**

String a cradle gym over her crib or cradle. Change the objects that are attached to the gym. Remember that the baby enjoys bright colors, interesting shapes, and things that move easily.

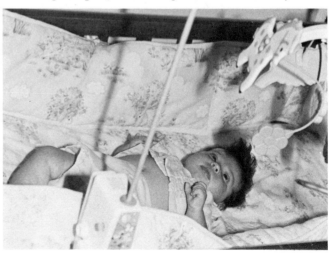

**Changing
Patterns**

Paste contact paper or wrapping paper with different colors and patterns on all sides of a diaper box. Loop a ribbon through the corner of the box and suspend it over your baby's crib. After a while your baby will reach up and bat at the box.

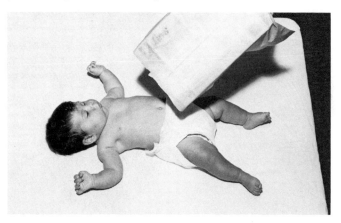

**Upside-Down
Daddy**

Lay baby on her back in Mother's lap. Let Daddy sit in a chair at right angles to Mother. This gives baby an interesting upside down view of Daddy's face.

**Give Baby New
Things to Look At**

Change the pictures on the wall by the crib or feeding chair. A pin-up board is ideal.

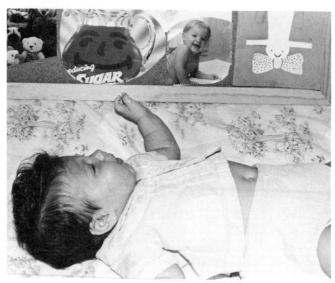

Listening:

Rattle Shake

Your baby is getting more efficient at tracking with her eyes and attending to different sounds. Let her practice these skills by moving a rattle at different speeds and in different directions as you sing this song:

Shake that rattle follow that sound.
Shake that rattle see what we found.
Shake it high and shake it low.
Shake it fast and shake it slow.
Shake that rattle follow that sound.
Shake that rattle see what YOU found.

(Give baby the rattle).

Up and Down

Sing songs to your baby that have up and down actions in them. As you move your baby up, down and around, she will see her world from different perspectives.

Here we go up, up, up (lift baby up).
Here we go down, down, down (put baby down).
Here we go front and back (turn baby around).
Here we go round and round (hold baby and spin around).

Calling Out to Baby

Call out to baby before you enter the room. Your baby will learn to recognize your voice and anticipate your arrival.

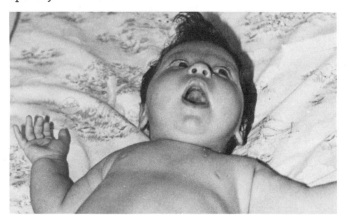

Let Baby Listen to Sound Cans

Make sound cans for your baby to listen to. Place sound cans first on one side of the crib and then on the other. After a while your baby will learn to search for the can with her eyes when she hears the sound. A bright swinging ribbon attached to the can makes it easier for your baby to follow.

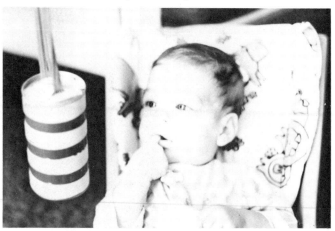

Feeling:

Rattle

Place a rattle in your baby's hand. Your baby will learn to recognize that the rattle is there. Sometimes she will shake it and sometimes she will bring it up to her mouth before she lets it drop. Be sure you give both hands a turn.

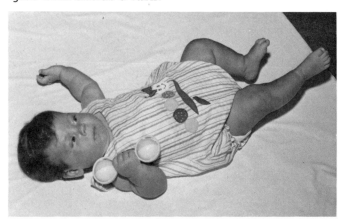

Feeling Sticks

Because baby's hands are open a great deal of the time, she will enjoy experimenting with different textures. Glue some textured fabric on old-fashioned wooden clothespins. Bits of burlap, satin, velvet or corduroy work well. These clothespins are ideal for encouraging grasping skills.

Exercising:

Pom Pom Toss

With your baby lying on her back in front of you, hold up large colored pom poms. Let them drop to her tummy and announce, "Here comes another pom pom!" As baby matures, she will begin to anticipate the pom pom falling.

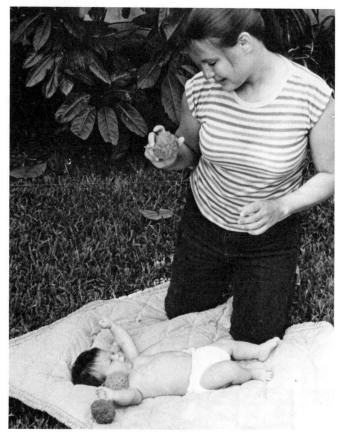

Move Baby's Legs as You Sing

Exercising baby's legs is important. Lay baby on her back. Hold her feet in the palms of your hands. Push them gently in a circular fashion. Soon she will be pushing *your* hands! Adding a song increases the fun!

Bicycle, Bicycle Baby (use your baby's name)
Bicycle, Bicycle girl
BOOP, BOOP (lift baby's bottom up by holding her feet)

Kicking Arena

The bottom of the crib provides an excellent rod for hanging an assortment of "kicking objects." Hang things at different lengths and try objects with different textures. A large pom pom and a bell provide baby with a soft quiet object and a hard, noisy object. Put baby on her back near the bottom of the crib so her feet can reach the kicking arena. Let her experiment.

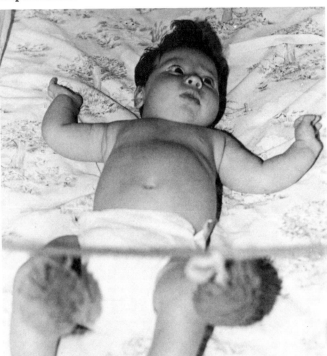

Daily Routines

Mealtime:

Play a Record

Play a special record to signal feeding time. Before long, the baby will learn what the record means.

Rocking Chair

If you haven't yet found how wonderful your rocking chair can be at feeding time, try it now. Holding your baby close, feeding and rocking are relaxing for you and baby.

Daddy's Turn

Make sure that Dad has some time to feed baby. If you are breastfeeding, let Daddy offer a water bottle if your baby drinks one. If you express your milk and need to go out during baby's mealtime, Daddy has the perfect opportunity!

Bathtime:

Let Baby Splash

Let baby splash her hands and feet in her warm bath water. Pat dry with towel after bath. Your baby learns about her world through her sense of feel.

Bathing Beauty

After your baby's bath, hold her up in front of a full length mirror. She will probably be attentive to this smiling figure. It's an excellent time for tickling her tummy and toes. As she looks in the mirror and feels your tickling, she is learning about herself.

More Massage

"Squeeze gently, twist gently" is a relaxing massage technique. With a small amount of vegetable oil in your hands, hold baby's leg up as if you were holding a baseball bat, and gently massage her legs. Massage her arms in the same way.

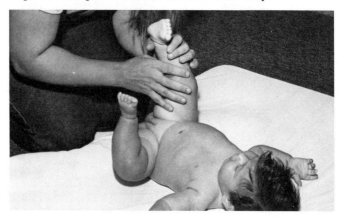

Diaper Time:

Feeling Mural

Hang a texture mural next to baby's table. A collage of materials will do just fine (towel, silky scarf, fuzzy wool, shiny aluminum foil). As you change baby, stroke her hands on the different textures and describe them to her.

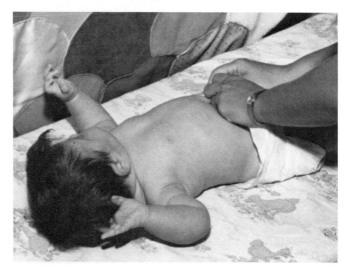

Look in the Mirror

Change baby near a mirror at times. Stick mirror wall tiles next to the changing table. Baby will be fascinated by her image. As she matures she will grow to enjoy this mirror play even more.

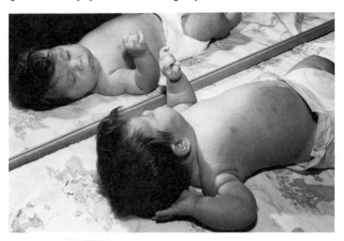

Feather Duster Fun

Keep an inexpensive feather duster near baby's changing table. While she is undressed, tickle her body parts as you name them.

Tickle, tickle, tickle
I tickle baby's nose today.
Tickle, tickle, tickle
We love tickle play.

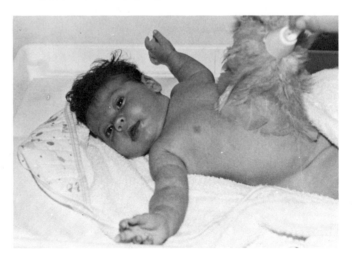

Punch Ball

Your baby spends a good deal of time on the changing table—probably looking at the white ceiling. Create an interesting, appealing environment for her by hanging an inflatable ball from the ceiling. At first your baby will watch it as it sways; soon she will make attempts to bat at it.

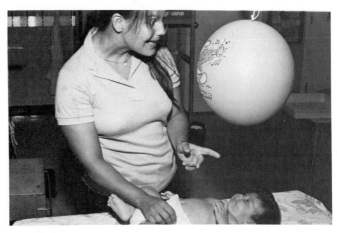

Quiet Time:

**Beach Ball
Baby**

Inflate a beach ball almost to its fullest capacity. Gently place baby face down on the beach ball, with tummy resting on the ball. Place your hands on her hips and slowly rock the baby back and forth. Many babies find this a relaxing activity that gets them ready for sleep.

T.V. Time

If your family enjoys watching T.V., your baby will enjoy sitting with you for a short period of time. She will enjoy the sound and movement, as well as the chance to be with the family.

Tape Your Baby's Sounds

If you happen to have a tape recorder, it's fun to use with the baby. Tape record the sounds your baby makes. Play back the tape to the baby often. Your baby may fall asleep as she talks along with the tape.

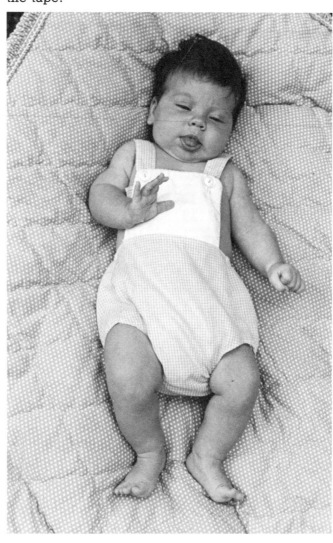

THREE MONTHS

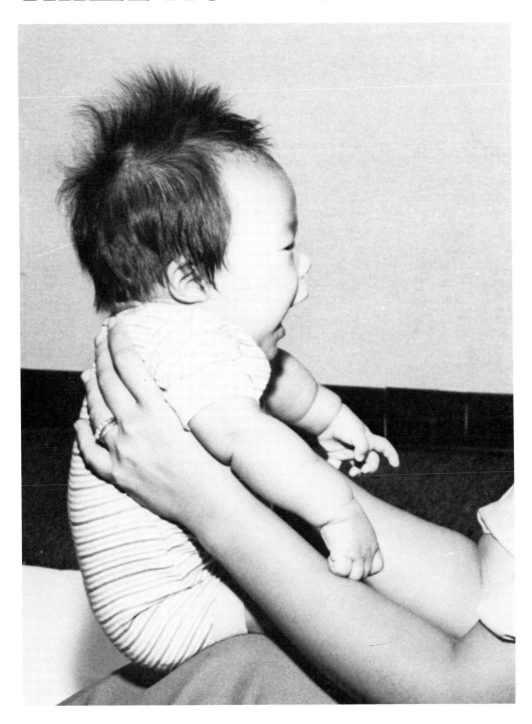

Baby's Viewpoint: The fourth month is exciting for baby and parents alike. As the infant spends more time awake each day, he has more time to explore his surroundings. His eyes catch sight of the mobile hanging over his crib. He looks from right to left, then left to right, and usually examines each piece. If his father moves a rattle across the crib, he follows it intently with his eyes. When it disappears from sight, baby continues to stare at the place where it was. Is baby registering surprise because it disappeared, or does he believe that looking will bring the rattle back?

Baby's favorite toy at this time is himself. He seems to be constantly trying to discover what he is, where he is, and what he feels like. His fingers explore his own eyes, nose, mouth and chin. He rubs his hand along his cheeks, patting, pinching and sometimes scratching. Many babies at this age will join their hands together and let each hand take a turn playing with the other.

In many ways the fourth month is a time of transition. In the first three months baby's primary energy is spent in self-regulation. His interaction with the world outside himself is focused on taking in information. He absorbs the world with eyes, ears, hands and mouth and is fascinated by his many discoveries. Now he is ready to explore his world in a more active way. He is getting ready to act upon—to be an impetus for action—a prime mover in a responsive environment. We see this first "action oriented" behavior in the baby's social world. He no longer waits to be spoken to and smiled at. He seeks out faces, then smiles and babbles, and makes the world smile back.

Motor Skills

An important "transitional" achievement that is likely to take place during the fourth month is the ability to sit with support. Sitting up instead of lying on back or stomach provides new opportunities for visual inspection. Just as important, it gives baby an opportunity to use his hands to manipulate toys.

The three month old begins to reach for objects although he is likely to miss the mark on the first try. Also, some time during the fourth month, most babies will bat at a cradle gym if it is strung over the crib. This batting activity follows a regular pattern. Baby bats at the gym, stops and then resumes his batting with increasing vigor.

Piaget, a Swiss psychologist who has studied infant behavior, suggests that the first time the baby bats at the gym it is accidental. But when he hits it, the gym moves up and down in an interesting way. The baby bats some more in order to make this interesting event happen again. In this effort to make something interesting happen again, we see the baby's growing capacity for purposeful behavior.

Differences in rates of development, particularly in the motor area can be very evident during the fourth month. While an active baby may already be turning from stomach to back, other babies are still limited to energetic bicycle movements with legs and arms. Because we can't always tell when a new skill will emerge, even the baby who hasn't learned to turn over should not be left alone on the changing table.

Seeing, Hearing, and Feeling

During the fourth month, baby shows an increased interest in his own hands and anything that they happen to be holding. He holds an object in view for a longer time now and inspects it with his eyes. Often he lies quietly on his back staring intensely, first at one hand, then the other. If you place a rattle in his hand, he will first look at it and then bring it up to his mouth. If you hold an object directly in front of him, he may grasp it with two hands.

Baby is really beginning, at the same time, to anticipate future events. Just a few weeks ago he continued to cry with hunger until the nipple was in his mouth. Now, as soon as he sees the bottle, he reacts. His crying may stop or may get louder. Baby is clearly attaching a meaning to a visual stimulus. The bottle he is looking at is more than a sensation. It is "something" that belongs in his mouth.

Along with this new awareness of the function of objects, there is a new reaction to objects that drop out of sight. Baby will follow a rattle that is taken away and then stare at the spot where it was last seen. He is holding on to a memory trace of his rattle, but he doesn't know yet that looking won't bring it back.

The three month old's impressive ability to hold onto a memory trace is demonstrated by his smiling behavior. In an experimental situation, babies as young as six weeks old will smile more for an animated, talking mother than an animated talking adult. The three month old continues to smile more for his parent than to a different adult, but at a new level of sophistication. Now baby smiles immediately at the appearance of his mother's face even when Mother is silent. Baby's smile is now more than a pleasant association, it is a smile of recognition.

Association between sight and sound is now mastered. Baby turns his head toward the sound of his mother's voice. A jingling rattle attracts his attention and he will turn his head completely around in order to keep it in sight. He particularly enjoys musical toys, radio, records, or even the beat of a metronome. He will turn toward the thing that makes the noise even when it isn't moving.

With his hand open most of the time now, baby uses his fingers for active exploration. The soft border of the blanket slips between his fingers and he rubs his thumb up and down to continue the pleasant sensation. The baby is no longer passively enjoying a variety of sensations. He actively selects the sensations he enjoys and provides his own pleasure.

Knowing Your Baby

By the fourth month, the infant has become quite a social being. His response to attention, his delight with imitative play, his active vocalizations, his out-loud chuckles, are all signs of a need and readiness for social interaction. It is during this period that parents and babies spend long periods of time talking back and forth with each other. Parent talks and smiles, and baby babbles and smiles back. An outsider watching this intense conversation will have difficulty deciding who in fact is the leader.

An outcome of these intimate conversations is a closer than ever bond between parent and child. Parents not only identify their own baby's different cries, they interpret a whole range of sounds that baby makes — a whimper of hunger, a laugh of delight, a gurgling of vocal play. Babies, in turn, are identifying parents by sight as well as feel. Although they are quick to return anybody's smile, the most radiant smiles are reserved for parents.

An exciting development between 3 and 4 months is a rapid increase in vocalization. Baby spends a lot of time practicing his newly found vocal talents. Now his vowel and consonant sounds are quite distinguishable and his repertoire may include sounds of "l"—"n"—"m"—"b"— and "p". His consonant sounds are produced most often when he is content and relaxed.

Babble conversations, although certainly an important developmental event, are not the only way you communicate with your baby. You and your baby are constantly sending messages back and forth to each other, through facial expressions, through body language, and through actions. One of the messages your baby may be communicating to you is, "Don't put me down, even if I am asleep, I need you." When your baby was younger we suggested that you respond to your baby without concern about "spoiling." We are still not concerned about spoiling a baby but do feel that it is important to help babies learn over time to acquire internal resources. In other words, just as your baby is sending out the message, "Don't put me down, I need you," you need to send a message back, "I am putting you down, and I love you and you're fine."

In an earlier chapter we talked about the importance of helping your baby accept a pacifier. Babies who enjoy a pacifier at three months have a ready-made self-comforting strategy that helps them settle down in a crib. Another way to help your baby accept the transition from your arms to the crib is to put him down in the crib when he is feeling relaxed and happy. As you place him in the crib continue talking and smiling, keeping your face close to his and maintaining eye contact. In a sense he can even read your facial expression. If you remain calm, cheerful and in control when you place your baby in a crib or infant seat, he will learn from you that he too is in control.

SUGGESTED ACTIVITIES
Setting the Stage

Give Baby a Cradle Gym

Baby is eager to practice his new batting skill. A cradle gym is an excellent toy at this time. The most effective cradle gym jingles and spins when the baby hits it. Position the baby so that he can activate the cradle gym with his arms and then with his feet. A disk with a face on it attached to the cradle gym makes the batting even more fun.

Take Baby Outside

Being outside is a wonderful change of scenery for you and your baby. Place the baby under a tree. He will enjoy listening to the rustle of leaves and watching the play of light and shadow as the leaves move with the wind. Birds give the baby practice in tracking and the cars and airplanes make novel and interesting noises.

Talk to Baby

Carry on conversations with baby at every opportunity. Use different tones of voice, high, low, loud, soft, laughing, soothing. When the baby "talks" to you, wait until his "sentence" is over and then imitate his sounds. The more you talk with your baby, the more babbling he will do. Use your baby's name frequently. When singing or reciting nursery rhymes, substitute your baby's name for the word "baby."

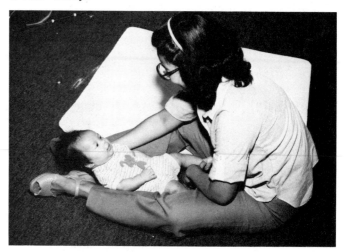

Invite a Guest

Invite another baby over to visit. Of course baby is too young to play with another but the babies will notice each other. At the same time you will enjoy sharing your observations with the other parent.

Singing Songs to Your Baby

During the first year, one of the activities that we suggest over and over again is singing to your baby. As your baby grows older you will find yourself changing the ways you sing with your baby. With the newborn you sang softly, steadily and held your baby close. Now you will find that your baby enjoys it most when you move closer and then further away.

Playtime

From birth to three months, the playtime activities we suggested were geared to practicing new skills in seeing, listening, feeling and body movement. Now, as your baby has become more adept at using his senses to explore his environment, playtime provides an opportunity to put his new skills to work. As he plays games and tries out activities, he will make discoveries, anticipate events, develop coordination, and solve new problems.

Making Discoveries:

Pet Watching

Let your baby have the opportunity to see your pet as it moves around. Dogs and cats and birds are especially exciting to watch.

New Perspectives

Lift the baby up and down in your arms so that he can watch your face from different perspectives.

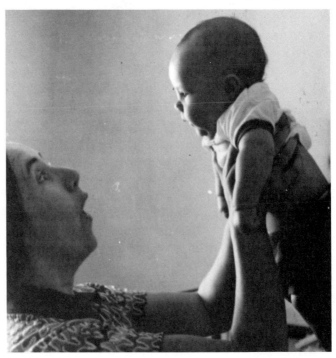

String Beads in Playpen

The playpen is an ideal spot for an infant during the fourth month. The baby has plenty of room to move and turn and toys can be placed within the baby's reach. String a spool necklace from one side of the playpen to the other. Baby will enjoy hearing the rattling as he kicks the necklace with his feet. (A spool necklace can also be strung between two chairs, if you don't have a playpen.)

Introduce Some Rhythms

Baby enjoys music and rhythm. Play a record with strong rhythm. Using a dapper clapper, a tamborine, two clothespins or your clapping hands, tap out the beat of the song. Try different songs, some fast, some slow, some loud, some soft. After a while, baby will recognize a marked change in the rhythm.

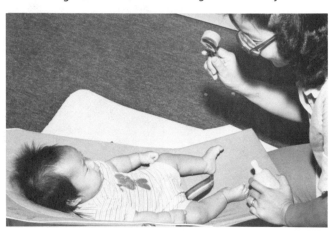

Shake-Shake

Place a wrist band with a bell sewn securely inside a fold on baby's wrist. Shake baby's hand gently until he begins to look at his hand. Change the wrist band to the other hand and repeat with more shaking. This activity increases body awareness and improves eye-hand coordination.

Safe Sandbox

Fill a large bowl with baby oatmeal. Place the bowl on a large tray or piece of plastic (to keep the area clean). Sitting on the floor with your baby in your lap, place his feet and hands in the raw oatmeal. Describe how it feels. Show him how you sift it through your fingers. Your baby will learn to enjoy new sensations.

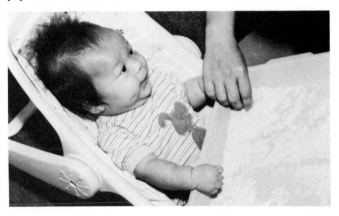

Buzzing Bees

To encourage more babbling, try singing this tune with your baby. Remember to maintain eye contact as you sing!

Ba Ba Ba Bumble Bee
First you say Ba to me
Then I say Ba to you
Ba Ba Ba Bumble Bee.

Give your baby a chance to respond with his own "b" sound!

Texture Glove

Make yourself a pair of texture gloves. Use an odd glove and tape a different fabric around each finger. Let your baby grasp each of the fingers.

Surprise Songs

Learn a variety of songs to sing to your baby that include a surprise ending. Through repetition, your baby will begin to anticipate the surprise. Try this one while baby is sitting on your lap:

(Bounce baby up and down on your knees.)
Trot trot to Boston
Trot trot to Lynn

(Open up your legs and catch your baby as he drops through.)
You'd better watch out or
You might fall IN!

Improving Coordination:

Play With Baby's Legs

Lift up the baby's legs and then let them fall as you recite:

Hippety Hippety Hippety-Hop
Hippety Hippety and then we flop.

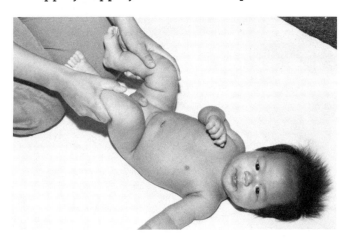

Play a Sit-Up Game

Pull the baby up gently and slowly by his arms in a "see-saw" game. Here's a chant to use with the game:

Up my little Kenneth comes
Down my Kenneth goes,
Peek around, have you found
Kenneth's wiggly toes.

The game strengthens the baby's stomach muscles and at the same time lets him see the world from different points of view.

Row Row Row Your Baby

Using this familiar verse, "Row, row, row, your boat," cradle your baby in your lap facing you. Support his back and head with your arms. Gently rock baby back and forth while singing.

Row row row your baby
Gently down the stream (hesitate with singing and motion)
Merrily, merrily, merrily, merrily -
Life is but a dream (resume rocking at a faster pace).

Push on Baby's Feet

Place the baby on his stomach on a hard surface. Standing behind him, place the palms of your hands against the soles of his feet. Your baby will ease himself forward by pushing first against one of your hands and then the other. Practice with this pushing exercise will get the baby ready to crawl on his own.

Roly-Poly

Between three and four months most babies are beginning to turn over. Usually babies begin by rolling from front to back. Next, babies will master back to side and finally from back to front. Help your baby practice these emerging skills. Put your hands under his shoulders. Gently rock him back and forth. When he is on his side, hesitate and let him try to turn himself the rest of the way over.

> Roly poly
> My little Erik,
> Roly-poly
> We'll have fun!
> Roly-poly
> My little baby,
> You have to roll before you RUN!

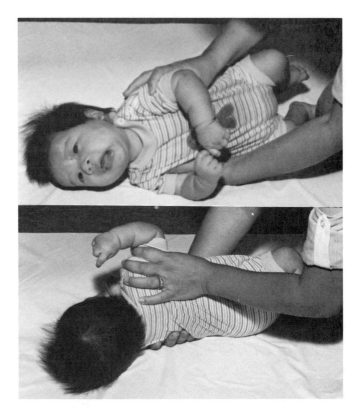

As you sing, roll baby back and forth to the rhythm of the music—any tune will do. At this age some babies wake themselves up at night because they flip over and can't flip back. Helping baby learn to roll over may solve this problem.

Solving Problems:

Put a Rattle in Baby's Hands

Continue placing a slim handled rattle in your baby's hands. Shake your baby's hand gently. See if he will lift his arm to see what is making the noise.

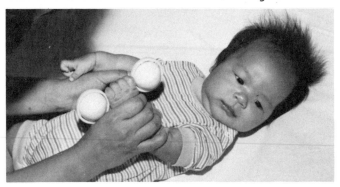

Tracking Fun

Lay baby on his tummy on the floor. Roll a bright, attractive ball from side to side about two feet in front of your baby. With a little practice your baby will be able to coordinate eye and hand movements, and reach toward the ball.

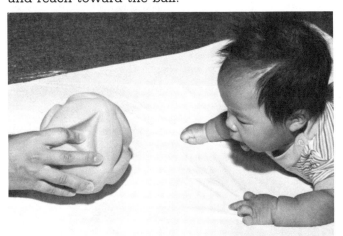

**Searching for
a Bell**

Ring a bell that makes a pleasant tinkling sound
while baby is watching. Sound the bell again on the
side just out of baby's line of vision. See if your baby
will search for the bell with his eyes. Try this game
with a rattle and a squeak toy.

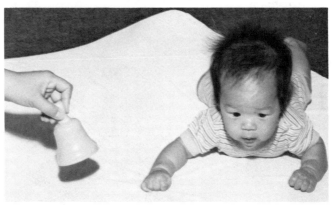

**Beach Ball
Batting**

Inflate a beach ball. Tie a string to the nozzle.
Lay baby on his back. Hold the beach ball above
baby's legs. Can your baby kick the ball with his
feet?

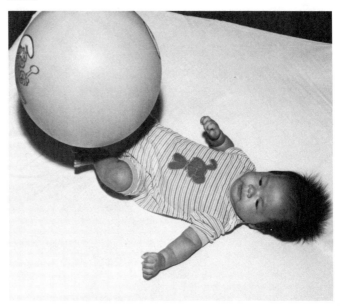

Merry-Go-Round

Put a bright ring on a string and circle it slowly in one direction around your baby's head. After a while, your baby will anticipate the ring's reappearance and search for it with his eyes.

Daily Routines

Mealtime:

Touching Time

Your baby needs to be held and cuddled as he eats. There's no place for bottle propping!

Make sure your baby's arms and hands are free to touch and explore as he is feeding. Encourage him to touch your face by gently rubbing your eyes, nose, mouth and hair with his hands.

Bathtime:

Make bathtime part of your baby's routine. A typical schedule might be bath, massage, dress, feed and sing to baby before you put him to sleep. Find the routine that works best for you and your baby.

Singing in the Bath

Use bathtime to further develop your baby's self-concept. Sing songs about his body parts as you wash them. Try this one for fun (to the tune of "London Bridge is Falling Down").

Head and shoulders, knees and toes,
knees and toes
knees and toes,
Head and shoulders, knees and toes,
Eyes and ears, and mouth and nose!

Play Ball

Put some brightly colored balls in baby's bath. As baby begins to regard them and reach for them, he will begin to get a sense of things that are slippery and wet, and things that float.

Bath Togetherness

For a relaxing change of pace, take a warm bath with your baby. Let baby experience your holding him on his back as you rock him back and forth. *Make sure you have someone to help you out of the tub. Wet babies are slippery!*

Diaper Time:

Naked Baby

Give baby opportunities to be without his diaper at times. Put him on a washable surface in case of an accident. Being naked allows baby to become more aware of himself. It's also a perfect time for some gentle massaging.

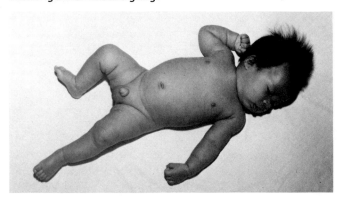

**After Bath
Exercise**

Use diaper time for more exercising with baby. Try singing this song as you move baby's body parts:

If you're happy and you know it,
kick your feet;
If you're happy and you know it
kick your feet.
If you're happy and you know it and
you really want to show it,
If you're happy and you know it
kick your feet.

Also, *clap your hands, find your nose, tickle your tummy,* etc.

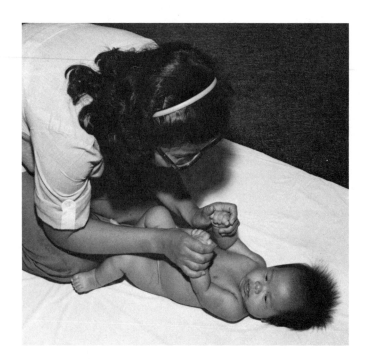

Animal Sounds

Whisper in baby's ear. Make different sounds, a moo, a bark, a meow, a peep, etc. He will notice the different sounds, smile, and perhaps even laugh aloud.

Quiet Time:

Watching Bubbles

Blow bubbles with liquid bubbles and a wand for your baby. Your baby will love watching the bubbles as they slowly float by.

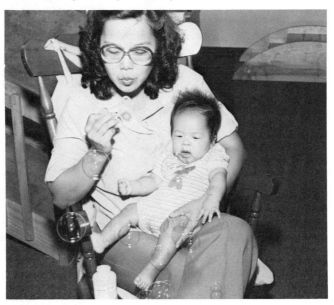

Phone Time

When you speak on the telephone, hold your baby close and look at him. Your baby will enjoy watching and listening to you—he'll even think your conversation is just for him!

Tick-Tock Goes the Clock

Let a clock tick near baby. The rhythmic ticking gives baby an awareness of rhythm and may help to soothe him.

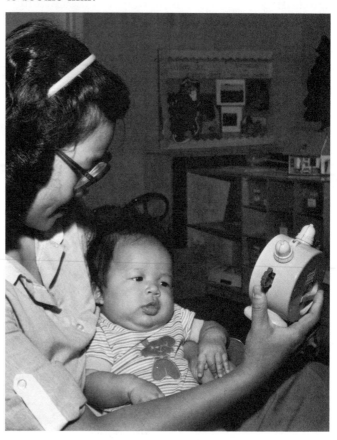

FOUR MONTHS

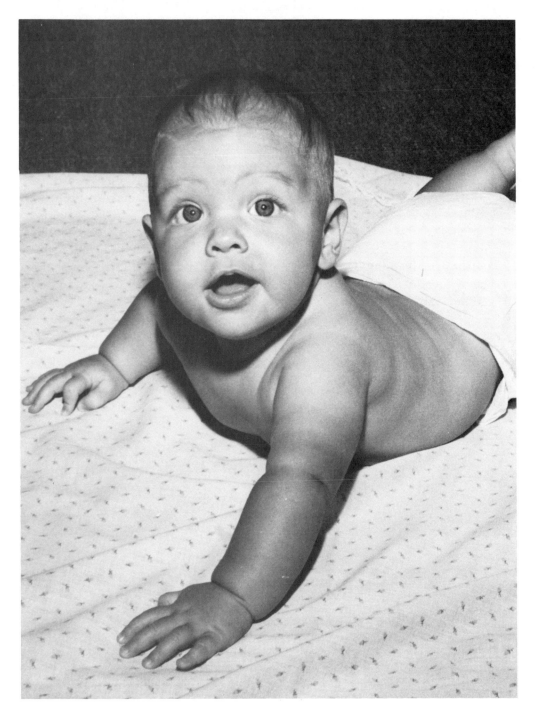

Baby's Viewpoint: By four months old your baby has made the transition from passive observer of interesting sights and sounds to active player. Now that she has learned to reach and grasp she seeks opportunities to practice her new-found skill. A mobile on her crib but out of reach is a source of frustration. She wants to bat it, grasp it, pull it to her mouth and then watch exciting things happen.

As you watch your baby playing with her mobile, you will discover that she is involved in a kind of routine. She grasps and releases the ring of the mobile, watches the mobile twirl, then attempts to grasp it again. This grasp, look, then grasp again routine is not, of course, limited to the mobile in the crib. Your baby is now ready to play with many toys. As she manipulates each new object within her reach, she is asking a wordless question. What is this thing in my hand and what can I make it do?

These new developments in your baby's interaction with objects are matched by the new developments we see in social interactions. The four month old is learning to initiate a social exchange. Instead of waiting for a visitor to make the overtures, the baby coos and babbles as soon as the visitor arrives. And because nothing is quite as captivating as a cooing smiling baby, the visitor is compelled to respond.

Motor Skills

For many babies, the fifth month marks the beginning of mobility. Some babies learn to crawl, stomach down, pulling along with their arms, bringing their legs up in a frog-like position and pushing forward with their feet. Other babies edge forward by pulling with only their arms. Often a baby will learn to crawl backwards before she manages to crawl forward.

Many babies can roll now from stomach-to-back. Some babies can also manage a back-to-stomach roll. Your baby now sits up quite successfully when propped on pillows, and may even take some tentative steps when held up. Contrary to popular belief, standing a baby on her feet before she can successfully bear her weight does not produce a bow-legged baby.

Baby's hands are now busy reaching and grasping. As long as your baby is able to see both her hand and the object at the same time, she is able to grasp at just about anything she sees. This grasp, however, is quite crude. The thumb and fingers are not yet "independent agents." Baby holds an object by pressing her fingers against the palm of her hand. An object lying on a table is scooped up rather than picked up.

As your baby practices her newly acquired grasping skills, she will spend relatively long stretches of time actively engaged in playing with a toy. A cradle gym stretched across her crib, with a dangling ring and a rattle-type toy, is especially attractive to her. As she grasps the ring, lets go, and grasps it again, her efforts are rewarded by the jingling of the rattle toy.

Seeing, Hearing, and Feeling

The four month old's improved eye-hand coordination is in part a reflection of improved visual skills. The younger baby's visual system, like a fixed focus camera, could see objects clearly only if they were 8–12 inches away. Now your baby can change her focus so that she sees things sharply at different distances. This newly acquired skill explains the excitement of visiting new places and seeing new sights.

A favorite toy at this age is a mirror. An unbreakable mirror hanging from a cradle gym or attached to the side of her crib is now a source of real pleasure. Baby catches sight of her own image in the mirror, watches the movements of her hands and face, and smiles at herself.

Despite baby's increased visual skill, her main means of exploring objects is with her mouth. She mouths an object as soon as she grasps it. Seeing, grasping and mouthing seem to happen in rapid succession. After a while she will add visual inspection to this routine. She will look at the object she has grasped before bringing it to her mouth.

Paralleling her new interest in visual exploration, is a fascination with new sounds. The four month old has discovered that she can make different kinds of sounds come out of her mouth and she enjoys listening to them. When she discovers a sound she particularly likes, a squeal, a bubbling, or a cough, she practices it over and over again. Many four month olds also experiment with changes in volume, babbling very loudly or softly and then listening to the effect they have created.

Knowing Your Baby

At four months old, babies are delighted with visitors and welcome a stranger with almost the same enthusiasm as they do a parent or sibling. As a matter of fact, they are delighted with faces in just about any form. The scariest looking mask or the oddest looking puppet are delightful playmates from the baby's point of view.

Although the four month old baby enjoys meeting new people, her way of interacting with new people is different from her way of interacting with Mom and Dad. Baby not only responds more enthusiastically to her parents' overtures, she also uses her fingers to actively explore their face. She touches eyes, nose, and moustache. She pulls at a strand of hair. And when her parents talk to her, she sticks her fingers inside their mouths as if physically capturing their words.

At the same time baby demonstrates this intense fascination with the words coming out of her parent's mouth, her own repertoire of sounds continues to expand. She masters most of the vowel sounds as well as a few of the consonants. At three months, babies of all languages and nationalities as well as deaf sound alike. By four months we begin to see a change as babies tune in to the language that they hear spoken. Sounds that they hear spoken are practiced.

Although a four month old baby may carry on a fine conversation with a bird mobile or a brightly colored rattle, she seems most enthusiastic when faced with a responsive audience. Mommy imitates her babbling sounds and baby's babbling increases in volume and intensity, with parent and child exchanging strings of high pitched, happy vocalizations. Parents heighten the excitement by first speeding up their rate of speaking, then slowing it down, only to speed it up again. Or they can alter their speaking volume and produce a similar effect.

Parents, especially fathers, respond to the baby's enthusiastic verbalizations by providing physical stimulation. They hold the baby in the air, tickle her tummy, or give her a noisy kiss. The baby is likely to respond to this intrusive stimulation with a burst of laughter. A surprise response from Mom or Dad, such as a cough or sneeze, will also initiate a chuckle.

Although the outloud laughter of a four month old baby is fun to listen to, it is important to remember that, in babies, laughter and fear are very close together. The baby's laugh serves as a release valve for mounting tension. If the tension is too great, however, the laughter changes to crying. You are likely to see this quick switch from laughter to tears in a rough house session with your baby. At one moment you lift your baby in the air and she laughs out loud. A second later, you lift her a little higher, and she burst into tears. For the young baby there is a fine line between enough and too much excitement. Parents become adept at knowing just how much stimulation their babies enjoy.

Setting the Stage

Baby Enjoys Being Up and About

Babies enjoy seeing the world from different perspectives. (When baby is sitting up, it's easier to talk with mommy and daddy and to watch their movements). Keep baby propped in a sitting position for part of every day. Try a bounce chair or an infant seat. As baby develops better balance she will be able to sit on the floor with pillows propped around her.

Baby Needs Some Time on a Flat Surface

Let baby play on a firm flat surface wearing only a diaper. Free from the restrictions of clothing and covers, she is able to perform her finest gymnastics.

Give Baby Practice Reaching

When baby is in the infant seat, hang up interesting toys on strings to encourage her to reach. Equip her crib or playpen with an interesting cradle gym. It's particularly fun when the toys make noise.

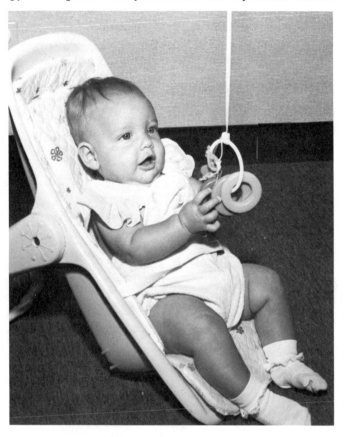

Give Baby Practice Grasping

Baby is refining her grasping skills at the same time she is practicing reaching. Have a supply of different size rattles available to help her practice. Hand a rattle to the baby first to her left hand and then her right hand. Hold it close to her and then make her reach for it. Hold the rattle higher, then closer, and then farther. As the baby practices her grasping, she gets better and better at coordinating her hands and eyes.

Door Swing

This is the perfect age to use a swing that hangs from a door frame. Your baby is strong enough to sit comfortably but not strong enough to try to get out. Baby will enjoy the back and forth movement of the swing while simultaneously carrying on a conversation.

Playtime

Now that your baby is spending more time awake, make sure that your baby has equal opportunities to play with toys as well as playing with people. Both kinds of experiences are important.

Making Discoveries:

Play a Game of Peek-a-Boo

Play peek-a-boo with the baby. Try placing your hands over your eyes, then over the baby's eyes. Place a blanket over your head and come out with "boo." The baby will enjoy all variations of the game.

Wheel a Toy Down a Hill

Build a cardboard "hill" in the baby's playpen. Let the baby watch a wheel toy slide down the hill. This provides an early lesson in cause and effect relationships.

Bubble Tracking

Your baby still enjoys watching bubbles float through the air. Blow bubbles when baby is outside in her walker. Baby will squeal with delight as she watches the bubbles float.

Use a Tape Recorder with Baby

Tape record your baby's babbling and play it back to her. Tape record Mommy's and Daddy's voice and play this back as well. See how your baby reacts when your voice comes from the tape recorder instead of from your mouth.

**Place a Face
Sock on Baby's
Foot**

Baby is now interested in discovering the parts of her own body. Put a brightly colored sock on your baby's feet. At first the baby will just look at her feet, but after a while she will succeed in catching a foot—a very important "conquest" in her young life.

Fabric Ball

Make a fabric ball by cutting several pieces of fabric into three inch strips. Tie the strips of fabric together and secure them in the center with an extra strip. Your baby will enjoy holding the ball and feeling the different textures. Fabric balls with bells inside are also fun and are sold in most stores that carry baby toys.

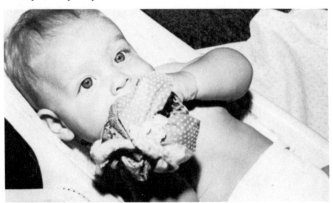

Improving Coordination:

Give Baby Some Rough-Housing

Mild rough-housing is very much in order now. Hold your baby at the waist, raise her in the air, jostle her up and down, then hold her upright in a standing position.

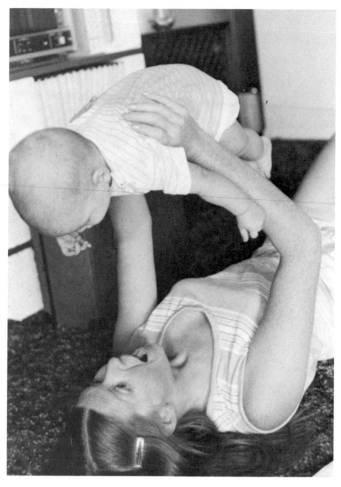

New Perspectives

Place a small pillow under the baby's tummy while she is on a rug. This will strengthen the neck and arm muscles.

Frog Kick

When baby is on her tummy:

1) Bend her knees up at the same time,
2) Separate her legs as you let her knees strengthen and
3) Pull her legs back together.

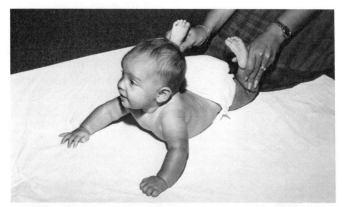

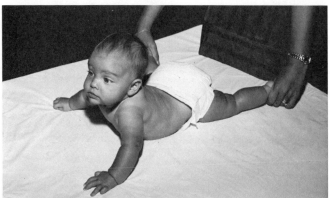

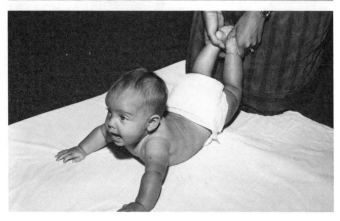

Here is a song to go with the exercise (to the tune of "Here We Go Looby Loo"):

We bend our knees like this
Now out to the side we go
We snap our legs together again
I love my baby so.

Quilt Roll

Spread a quilt in the grass and lay your baby on her stomach along one side of the quilt. Gently raise the quilt to help your baby roll from her stomach to her back. Reward her efforts with a kiss and a hug.

Move Hands Up and Down

Move the baby's hands up and down, in and out, as you recite this jingle.

Up-up-up
My baby goes
Reach way up
And touch your nose

Down-down-down
My baby goes
Reach way down
Touch baby's toes

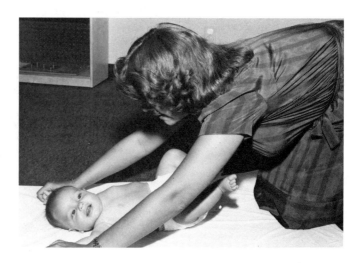

Place Toys Out of Reach

If your baby has learned to move by squirming or crawling, place toys just out of her reach. She will discover that she has to both wiggle and reach in order to get the toy. Be careful not to frustrate her. If she doesn't reach the toy within a few seconds, put it within her reach.

Exercise Baby While You Sing, "The Wheels on the Bus"

Lay baby on her back. Sing this song while putting baby through the following motions:

The wheels on the bus go round and around (roll baby's arms)
Round and around
Round and around
The wheels on the bus go round and around, all over town.

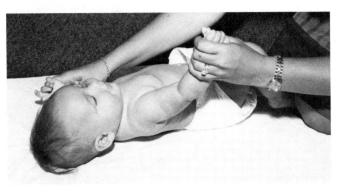

The people on the bus go up and down (baby's arms go up and down)
Up and down
Up and down
The people on the bus go up and down, all over town.

The wipers on the bus go swish, swish, swish (hold baby by the hips and gently roll her back and forth)
Swish, swish, swish
Swish, swish, swish
The wipers on the bus go swish, swish, swish, all over town.

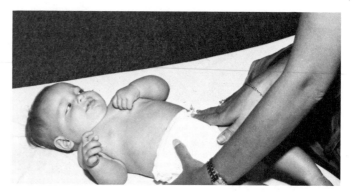

Continue other verses, repeating sound and motions:

The horn on the bus goes beep, beep, beep (press baby's tummy). . . .

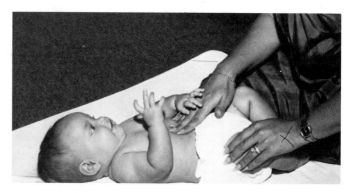

The ride on the bus goes bum bum bump (gently
bounce baby). . . .

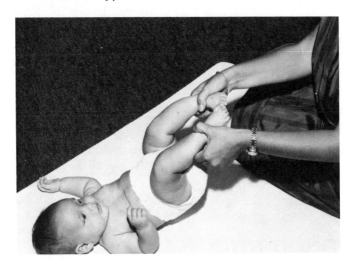

**Keep
Practicing
Songs from
Earlier Months**

Remember your baby enjoys the familiar as well
as the new. Sing some songs from earlier months
like, "Here We Go, Up-up-up," or "Row, Row, Row
Your Boat."

Solving Problems:

**Give Baby Two
Latex Toys**

Give your baby two squeak toys, one for each
hand. Make sure that they are made of soft latex so
that your baby can squeak the toy with just one
hand. Watch to see if your baby will look at the hand
that is doing the squeaking. When she gets a little
older she will learn to squeak with both toys at the
same time.

Scarf Bracelet

Attach a plastic bracelet to a colorful silk scarf, and tie the scarf around the arm of a chair. Your baby will grasp the ring and watch the scarf move up and down. Soon she will discover different ways to make the scarf move.

Curtain Ring Collision

Make a simple chain by tying curtain rings together. Tie them on the crib or the back of a chair where your baby can make them swing. Your baby will discover that a big swing creates a collision and a delightful tinkling sound.

Daily Routines

Diaper Time/ Bath Time:

Double Rattles

Tie a ribbon around the center of each of two dumbbell rattles so that the rattles are about three inches apart. Let your baby hold on to one of the rattles. Trying to catch the other rattle will keep her very busy while you are changing her diaper.

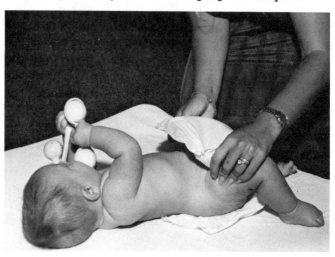

Play This Little Piggy Went to Market

Baby is discovering that she has feet. Help her become more aware of her body by playing this game before you dress her.

This little piggy went to market
This little piggy went home
This little piggy had roast beef
This little piggy had none
This little piggy went whee
Whee whee all the way home.

To Strengthen Baby's Back and Abdominal Muscles

While baby is undressed on the changing table lightly run your fingernails across her stomach. Observe how baby contracts her muscles in response. Turn baby on her stomach and run your fingernail down her spine. Baby will arch her back and lift her head.

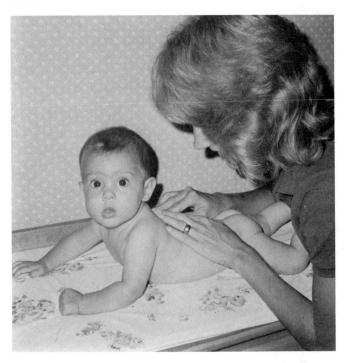

**Baby Powder
Rub**

After her bath your baby will enjoy having a powder rubdown. Talk softly to baby as you gently massage her body. Sprinkle the powder on your hands rather than sprinkling it directly on your baby. This will assure that your baby does not inhale the powder.

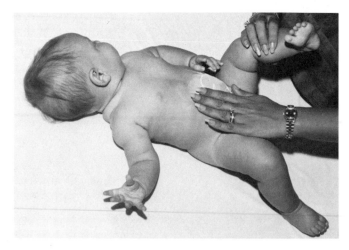

Mealtime:

**Showing the
Spoon**

If your baby has begun eating solids, make sure she sees the spoon before it goes into her mouth.

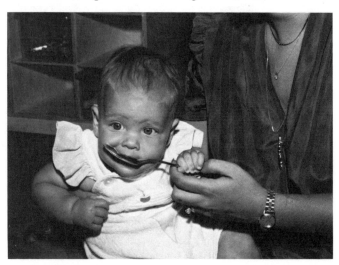

**Exercising Lips
and Tongue**

Put a little drop of food on baby's lips. As baby tries to lick it off she is getting her tongue in shape for babbling.

Quiet Time:

Huggee

Place a soft doll or stuffed animal in baby's crib. Always use the same doll. Baby will learn to associate the "huggee" with falling asleep.

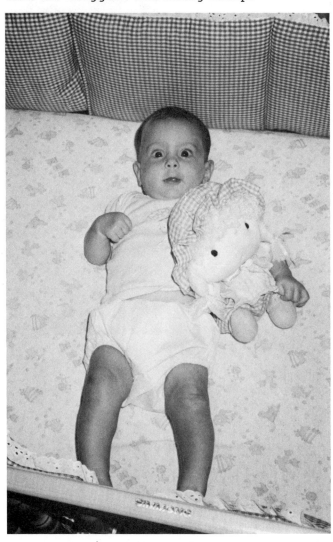

Hammock Ride

Swinging in a hammock with your baby in your arms is wonderfully relaxing for both you and your baby.

Lullaby

Babies really enjoy the lulling rhythm of a lullaby. Sing the same lullaby for naptime and sleeptime at night. Your baby will recognize the lullaby as a comforting sleeptime ritual.

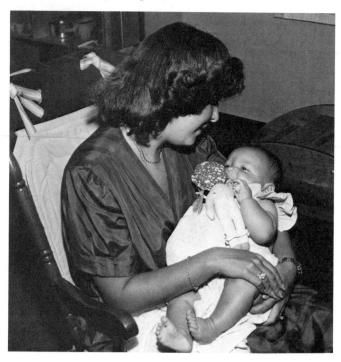

FIVE MONTHS

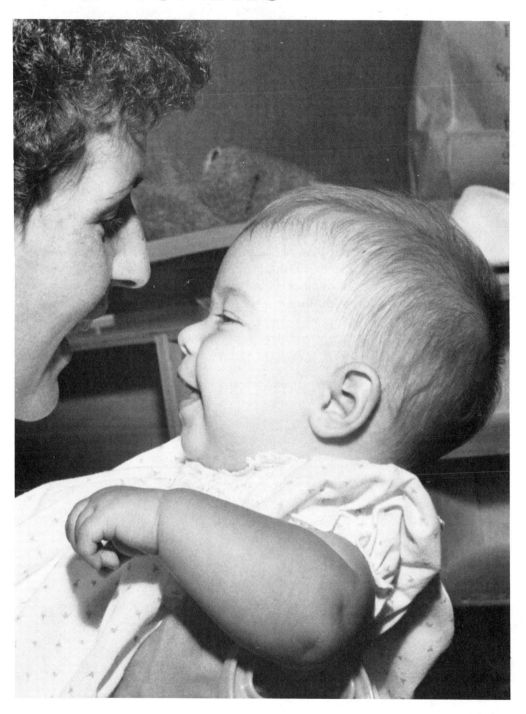

Baby's Viewpoint: Baby keeps his hands busy during most of his waking hours. He can not only scoop up a rattle or a ring, but can also release it at will. If a toy happens to be out of his reach, he looks at the toy and opens and closes his hand in a kind of abbreviated, almost symbolic, movement. It is as if the rattle by now has developed a special meaning. "A rattle is something to grasp, to hold, and to shake." The baby is trying to make sense out of his world. He has learned to define the things around him by what he can do to them.

Although the five month old warms up to strangers quite quickly, he makes a clear distinction between people he knows and people who are new to him. In a strange situation the baby is likely to cling to a familiar person. When he is tired, hurt, or fussy no one can soothe him as easily as his parents.

As we watch the baby's reactions to new people and new experiences, we recognize that the baby's emotional states are becoming more differentiated. The younger baby's emotional repertoire included a continuum of emotions between happy and unhappy. By the age of five months, happiness appears in more distinct forms, like excitement, joyfulness and quiet contentment. Unhappiness includes wariness, sadness and anger. And along with this increased repertoire of emotional states comes a new ability to use babbles to communicate feelings. The baby can now send out babble messages that mean "look at me," "pick me up," and "I don't like it."

Motor Skills

Differences in the rate of motor skill development are quite apparent at five months old. While some five month olds are crawling efficiently around the house, others will not begin to crawl for several months. It is important to remember that accelerated motor development is not necessarily associated with greater intelligence.

Whether a five month old baby is crawling or not, he is likely to enjoy an activity that allows him to push with his feet. With the help of a parent he may want to push himself up to a standing position. While lying in the bathtub he may enjoy pushing against a parent's hand and propelling himself through the water. A jump chair is especially popular. Baby loves to push against the floor with his feet and bounce himself up and down. Make sure that the jump chair you use is strong and well balanced. A robust baby, in a active moment, can tip his jump chair over.

At five months, most babies are quite adept at reaching and grasping. This feat can be performed with one hand and then the other. Most babies have also learned to rotate their wrists in order to inspect the object they have grasped. This wrist rotation, combined with a new ability to use his thumb and fingers cooperatively, makes it easier for baby to pick up small objects and even hold a spoon.

Baby seems to realize now that there are two sides to his body. Some babies are able to hold a toy in one hand, transfer it to the other, and then change back again.

As baby looks from one hand to the other, or passes a rattle from hand to hand, he is just as interested in what his hands are doing as he is in the toy itself.

Seeing, Hearing, and Feeling

"Seeing" plays a central role now in baby's exploration of objects. At first, baby batted at things because he wanted something exciting to happen again. Next, he used his grasping skill to get objects into his mouth. Now, at five months old, baby appears to be grasping in order to see. The rattle in his hand is twisted, turned and carefully inspected before it finds its way into his mouth.

As baby takes visual stock of his environment he devotes particular attention to following the movements of his mother. When mother steps out of the room, baby continues to gaze for a long time at the spot where mother was. As she steps back into the room, he follows every movement with his eyes.

At five months old, the baby will not only turn his head toward a sound, but will follow sound in a darkened room. He is particularly sensitive to the sound of footsteps and becomes alert and attentive when somebody enters the room. His interest in the sounds he can make continues. He may even have discovered how to change his own sounds by babbling with a finger or a toy in his mouth. He loves to listen to music and often becomes more active when the music is rhythmic and lively.

By the sixth month, bath time may become one of the highlights of the day. Most babies by now have discovered how to splash and will start a splashing game as soon as they get in the water. This game usually involves batting the water with both hands. When he is really going at it, baby will splash water in his own face and eyes, scream with surprise, and then go back to his splashing. He seems to be trying to find out whether his splashing has something to do with the water that gets in his face.

As well as providing the baby with an opportunity to splash, the bath is a good time for baby to investigate his own body. Supported by his parents' arms, the baby is in a good position for reaching his toes. After playing for a while with his slippery toes the baby is likely to discover his genitals. Then during drying time, he may discover his navel, or content himself with a tactile investigation of his nose and ears. If your face is close enough he may inspect your face too, as if trying to make a comparison.

Knowing Your Baby

Baby has now mastered many of his consonant sounds, including Ma-Ma, Da-Da, and possibly Na-Na. Interestingly enough, he almost never utters a single syllable—it is never just Ma, but always Ma-Ma, or Ma-Ma-Ma-Ma. When baby makes meaningful sounds such as Ma-Ma or Da-Da, his parents and brothers and sisters inevitably catch it and repeat it, showing their obvious delight. Baby responds to their enthusiasm by repeating those syllables over and over again. It is this sort of "reinforcement" that eventually turns babbling into talking.

Although the five month old baby does not not associate meaning with his babbles, even when they sound like words, he does learn to use language for his own purposes. He finds ways of calling his mommy into the room and ways of bringing her back when she starts to turn away. By responding to baby's call, Mommy is teaching her baby the power of language.

When Mom or Dad return to the baby after a brief separation, the five month old welcomes their return with an array of greeting behaviors, waving his arms like a windmill, bouncing up and down, calling out with loud excited coos. Siblings and other familiar persons are also likely to receive a welcome, although it may not be quite so exuberant.

The five month old is able to express his displeasure with the same intensity that he expresses delight. With a younger baby we see the expression of rage as a response to physical restraint. Now at five months old, the baby becomes enraged if he doesn't get what he wants. Taking away a toy, putting baby down before he's quite asleep, taking too long to put on a diaper, all can produce strong expressions of outrage.

SUGGESTED ACTIVITIES
Setting the Stage

Take Mobiles Down

Take down any remaining "touch me not" mobiles that baby keeps trying to reach. Baby is no longer contented with looking at interesting things. He wants to grasp, feel, twist, turn and examine. If the mobile that baby keeps reaching toward is not baby-proof, you are better off putting it away.

Front Baby Carrier

Baby slings that attach in front are better for taking baby out, because he can see your face when you talk to him.

Carry Baby Papoose-Style

Carry the baby on your back (papoose-style), while you are doing household chores.

Talk to Baby as You Move Him Around

Tell baby when you are going to pick him up, put him down, change his diaper, or place him in the bath or car seat. Even before baby can understand specific words he will learn that you are giving him a signal that a change is about to occur.

Hold Your Arms Out to Baby

Whenever you are about to pick up the baby hold out your arms and say, "Up." After a while baby will stretch his arms out toward you.

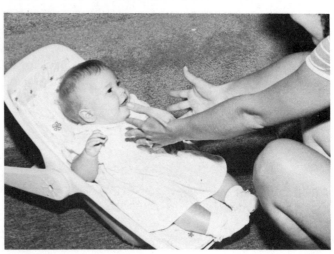

Playtime

Making Discoveries:

Give Baby a Shiny Pan

Give the baby a large shiny pan he can see himself in. Let him pat it, roll it, bang it. The baby loves to play with Mommy and Daddy's "toys."

Hold Baby in Front of a Mirror

Hold the baby up in front of a full-length mirror. Give him an opportunity to observe and respond to his own image. Point out Mommy and Baby in the mirror.

Keep Several Toys in Baby's Crib

Keep a collection of small toys in the crib with the baby. The baby will learn to tell his toys apart, and even choose a favorite toy or recognize a new toy that has been placed in his crib.

Roly-Poly Toys

This is an ideal age for a roly-poly toy. Your baby's major interest now is making discoveries about interesting objects. A roly-poly doll that rights itself when baby knocks it over provides a "maintenance free" toy that responds to your baby's actions.

Swing-a-Baby

Place the baby in an infant swing. As you push the swing away say, "Goodbye." As the swing comes back to you say, "Hello." Although the baby is too young to understand the words, he will recognize that you are using two different words. After a while your baby will be able to recognize that different sounding words have different meanings.

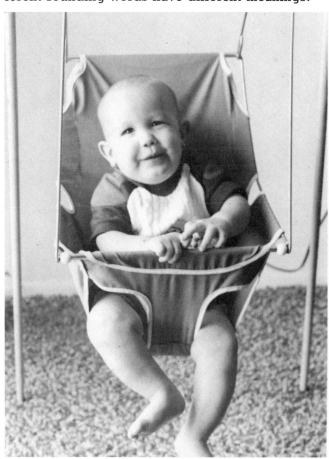

**Touch That
Sound**

As your baby begins to experiment with his voice, you will notice several distinct sounds: b, m, d, ah, ee, and oo. It is fun to imitate. While you make a sound, place baby's fingers on your lips. Let him feel the vibrations as each sound is made.

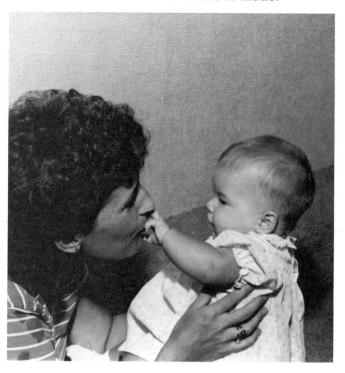

Rattles

Because the rattle is thought of as an "old-fashioned" toy, many babies are not given opportunities to play with rattles. This is a mistake. The folk wisdom that created that rattle is as valid now as it was a hundred years ago. At five months old the baby is beginning to learn "the schemas of objects." He is discovering that certain actions in his repertoire belong with certain objects. Because shaking is an early action schema, babies seem to automatically shake a rattle when it is placed in their hands. The more opportunity your baby has to try out different rattles, the more fun he has practicing his shaking skill.

Improving Coordination:

Play "How Big is the Baby?"

When your baby is sitting in the high chair or propped up in a sitting position, hold his hands down while you ask, "How big is the baby?" Then, as you raise his arms over his head, add the words, "SO BIG." If your baby responds with a laugh, you'll know he likes the game.

Play a Bouncy Game

Babies enjoy a song or rhyme while being bounced on Mommy or Daddy's knee. Rhymes with a "surprise" ending are particularly fun. Baby will learn to anticipate the ending activity and will let you know by smiling or laughing *before* the end comes. This shows the baby's increasing memory.

Try:

Baby be nimble, one, two, three
Baby jump onto my other knee.

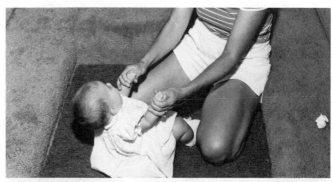

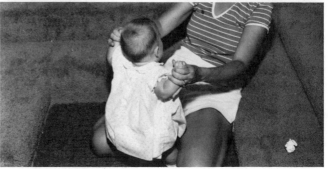

Ups-a-Daisy

Now that your baby has become adept at sit-ups, you might find that he is ready to try some beginning standing. You do have to remember, of course, that babies learn to straighten their knees before they learn to relax them. If your baby is ready to turn sit-ups into stand-ups, be sure to support your baby under the armpits. This way your baby can experience the fun of standing up without getting overtired.

Attach Rings to Crib Head

Attach rings to the head of the crib. The baby will learn to grasp the rings and pull himself forward.

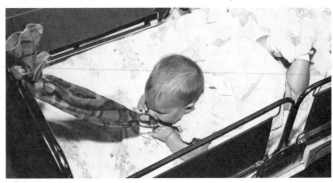

Baby Roll

If your baby has mastered rolling over, and if weather permits, place your baby outside on a blanket on a slight incline. Encourage your baby to roll down the incline.

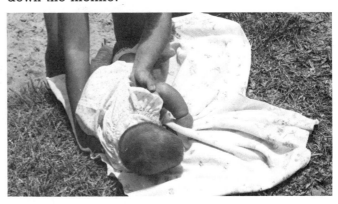

Tube Tumble

Inflate a pool tube. Place it around baby's waist while he is in a sitting position. If baby tumbles the tube will cushion his fall.

Solving Problems:

Hand Toys to Alternate Hands

Hand the baby a toy, first one hand and then the other. Soon the baby will learn to transfer the toy from one hand to the other.

Play Ball-Bouncing Games

Bounce a large ball up and down while the baby is watching. He will get better and better at following the bounce with his eyes.

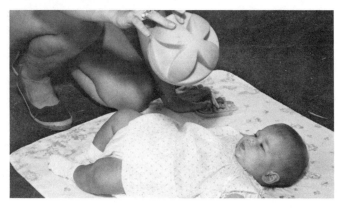

"Face-Sheet"

Faces continue to fascinate the five month old baby. Make a face out of fabric and sew it on the underside of his sheet. Baby will lift up the sheet and discover the smiling face.

"Turnabout"

Baby can tell the difference now between a face that is drawn properly and a face that is distorted. Using a very sturdy paper plate, crayon a smiling face on one side, and a distorted face on the other side. (Put in extra eyes, or change the position of eyes and mouth.) Once your baby discovers the two faces he may attempt to turn over the plate. Which face does your baby prefer to look at?

**Disappearing
Ball**

Roll a ball under a chair that is up against a wall, so that the ball hits the wall and comes back. See if your baby watches for the ball to come back.

Daily Routines

Mealtime:

**Give Baby His
Own Spoon**

Give the baby his own spoon during feeding time. Your baby will be less likely to reach for your spoon. But don't expect him to feed himself yet. Just holding on to a spoon is an accomplishment in itself.

Give Baby a Cup

Allow the baby to hold a cup. Some babies enjoy drinking from a cup at five months. At first put just a drop of water or juice inside to reduce the amount of spilling.

**Name the Parts
of Baby's Body**

As you dress or bathe baby make up little rhymes about his eyes, nose and mouth. Try out this rhyme:

What a surprise,
I'm washing your eyes
And this I suppose, is a nose.
And right under here, I've discovered an ear.
But where, oh where, are your toes?

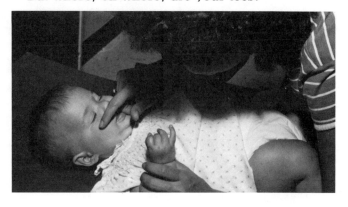

Stone Face

In the middle of a diaper time conversation, stop talking and keep your face perfectly still. Observe baby's efforts to get you going again.

Put a Boat in Baby's Bath

Placing boats in the bath with your baby will make bath time more fun. You can make an instant fleet out of plastic butter containers.

Quiet Time:

Pat-the-Baby

When you feel that your baby is getting tired, but can't quite settle down, hold him against your shoulder, and pat him gently and rhythmically. He will relax along with you.

Whisper to Baby

Whisper to the baby. As you find new ways to communicate with your baby, feelings of intimacy are fostered.

Swaying

Babies love to sway back and forth while being held tightly in Mommy and Daddy's arms. Sing to baby while you're swaying.

Brian is gently swaying, swaying, swaying, swaying

Brian is gently swaying, swaying, swaying
Swaying in the breeze.

SIX MONTHS

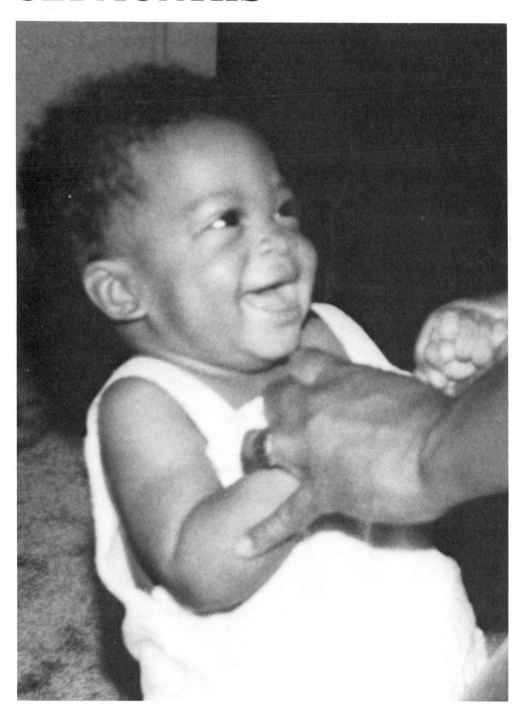

Baby's Viewpoint: The parents of a six month old may notice a subtle change in their baby's personality. Their nice, outgoing baby is becoming more fearful of new people. When a visitor approaches, her ready smile is not quite so ready. A grandmother who has been a consistent visitor may meet resistance when she tries to pick up her granddaughter. Fortunately, the baby's initial shyness tends to be shortlived. A little time and a shared toy overcome the shyness, and before long grandmother or visitor are treated as welcome playmates.

Why does this subtle change take place? Has baby really lost her easy-going disposition? Quite the reverse—baby's demonstrated preference for her parents is an overt expression of love. She has learned to associate Mommy and Daddy with safety, comfort, nurturance and pleasure, and she does not want a substitute. A new person could signify a temporary separation from her parents.

Once a baby has gotten used to a new visitor, she is apt to be a very good entertainer. The six month old is becoming aware of herself and her effect on other people. She will act silly or play the clown and get even sillier when her antics produce a laugh.

Motor Skills

At six months, many babies have learned to sit up by themselves, with their hands planted firmly on the floor in front of them to help them hold their balance. This independent sitting gives them a new perspective on the world. It is a perfect age for grocery shopping. Poised in the "jump seat" in the front of a grocery cart, the baby is at the center of a new universe full of bright colors, clanging noises, and bustling activity.

During the seventh month many babies are becoming quite mobile. Some are scooting around on their stomachs, using legs as pushers and arms as pullers. Other babies may be creeping around on their hands and knees, with stomach well off the floor. By the same token, some six month old babies who are also developmentally on target appear riveted to the floor. If you place a toy in front of them they strain to reach with their arms. Unsuccessful, they will dig their feet into the carpet in an attempt to lurch forward. Unfortunately these efforts are of no avail, and they end up further from their target than when they started. Often, we find that a baby who is especially well balanced in a sitting position will show no interest in crawling.

Grasp and reach are very precise now. Baby can grasp a toy with either hand, transfer a toy from one hand to the other, and then reach out with her empty hand to grasp a second toy. However, if you present her with a third object when both hands are full, she may have a problem. She wants the new toy but doesn't realize that her hand is too full to grasp it. In all probability, she will reach for the third toy and accidentally drop the second. It will take a while for your baby to learn how to put the second toy down, in anticipation of picking up a third one.

Along with her increased efficiency in reaching out for objects, baby is getting better at picking up small objects from the floor. Apparently, two things are happening. In the first place, she is learning to use her thumbs as well as her fingers so that she can get a better hold on things. In the second place, an increase in eye muscle efficiency gives her improved depth perception so that her eye and hand movements are better coordinated. This is the age when baby will struggle to pick up a crumb of bread, a speck of dust, or even the design of the sheet.

Your baby also shows a greater appreciation of depth perception. In a classic experiment, a psychologist demonstrated that a six month old child would not crawl over a bridge to her mother when there was an illusion of a drop off. In a real situation, six month olds are likely to stop at the edge of a bed or the top of a stairwell before taking a plunge. Unfortunately, there is no guarantee that the baby will exercise caution, so parents must stay on the alert. The fact that this distant depth perception appears at approximately the same time as creeping provides evidence of the synchrony, or basic groundplan, that underlies development throughout the first year.

At six months, many parents are interested in teaching their baby how to swim. The rationale is that swimming is like creeping and if a child is able to creep, she will be able to swim. Actually, whether the child is taught by a loving parent or a trained instructor, babies are able to hold their breath and paddle in the water for only a short distance. Few babies achieve the skill of lifting up their heads to take another breath and, with almost no exceptions, a six month old cannot swim purposefully from one spot to another. As long as the parent and baby are having a good time in the water, swimming is excellent exercise. There can be a problem with the "sink or swim" approach in that the baby may develop a fear of water that is hard to overcome.

Seeing, Hearing, and Feeling

At six months, baby is able to recognize many different sounds and sights. She pays attention to relatively small details and can tell the difference between a happy and a sad face. Baby enjoys playing with lots of different objects at the same time and particularly likes objects that combine sight, sound and touch appeal. A ball with different textures, a soft rubber toy with a loud squeak, blocks with bells inside, keys, spoons, pots and pans, and bright colored old-fashioned clothespins are all favorite toys at this age.

Now that the baby can sit with support and grasp efficiently, her interest in playing with toys has reached a new peak. Although she tends to focus on only one toy at a time, she has learned a set of actions that she uses with each one. When she picks up a rattle she is likely to start off her play by inspecting it with her eyes. A second or two later she shakes it vigorously, then fingers it with her other hand, bangs it against the floor, mouths it for moment, shakes it again, and then lets it drop. Moments later she might pick up a toy with quite different properties and put it through a similar set of tests.

Baby's interest in different sounds makes wrapping paper very exciting. She loves to crinkle tissue paper or squash tin foil. Because baby's exploration might involve stuffing the paper in her mouth, her paper playing activities have to be supervised. Don't let the baby put newspaper or magazines in her mouth. The ink contains a dye that could be harmful.

A major development at this age is the ability to recognize a familiar object when it is partly covered up. When a cloth is placed over her rattle so that it is partly hidden from view, baby will reach for her toy with obvious excitement. It seems that baby is getting closer to realizing that an object can exist, even when it is partly covered up. She still, however, is unlikely to search for her rattle if it is totally hidden. One explanation is that baby does not understand that objects continue to exist when they are not seen or felt. Another explanation is that baby does not realize that one object can be inside, underneath, or behind another.

Knowing Your Baby

Despite her wariness of strangers, the six month old is quite a sociable youngster. She loves to play with her sisters and brothers, or visit other babies. When two six month old babies are put together, they notice and imitate each other. If one laughs, so does the other. If one cries, the other does too. It seems as if the baby identifies with a playmate without really recognizing that her playmate is a baby like herself.

The mirror is now one of baby's favorite toys. She will sit herself in front of a long mirror and talk to and even kiss her own reflection. When her image remains silent, she may pat the mirror as if to investigate the problem.

As she gets better at holding images and sound patterns in her head, her repertoire of back and forth games increases. She anticipates the climax of "I'm going to get you," and laughs out loud before the tickling begins. A version of peek-a-boo in which Dad peeks back and forth from behind a door can elicit peals of laughter. When the adult grows tired of a back and forth game and decides to end it, the baby may have a different idea. As Dad rests his knees from "Trot, trot, to Boston," baby bounces herself up and down to make the game continue.

Baby's efforts to make an adult resume a game suggest that the baby is beginning to make some important distinctions between people and objects. "People, not objects, make things happen." Baby "talks" to toys in a conversational babble that does not require a response. The babble that is reserved for people is much more varied and interesting. It can sound like a question, an answer, a comment, or a command. If Daddy attempts to put the baby down when the baby does not want to be put down, the ensuing babble is most definitely a command.

Your baby at six months old is learning to imitate the phrase patterns of the language that is spoken around her. Her babbling begins to sound recognizable even when it isn't. In a way of speaking the Chinese baby babbles in Chinese, the Cuban baby babbles in Spanish, the American baby babbles in English, and the hearing impaired baby babbles less and less.

The baby also demonstrates a broader ability to imitate actions. Earlier imitation consisted mainly of facial expressions, vocalizations and other aspects of communication. Now we see evidence of the baby imitating the hand movements of other people. This imitation is limited to copying actions that the baby already knows how to do. It also requires that the baby see the part of her body that is doing the imitating. The baby may clap her hands in imitation, or bang on a pan after seeing a parent perform the same action.

SUGGESTED ACTIVITIES

Setting the Stage

Child-Proof Your House

If your baby is beginning to be mobile, "baby-proofing" is a necessity. Put gates across steps and staircases, close bathroom doors, plug-up outlets, check for sharp corners, and place baby-locks on cabinets. Remember—never take a chance! All poisons, cleaning fluids and medicines should be kept out of reach.

Get on the Floor With Baby

Babies at this age need a lot of "floor time" to help develop crawling and creeping skills. If your baby doesn't enjoy being on the floor by herself get down and play with her.

Keep Baby's Toys in Small Baskets

Your baby may be beginning to take an interest in small toys and containers. Store her favorite things in a small basket and let her get things out herself. Several smaller baskets are preferable to one large toy chest.

Name Things for Baby

During the last few months you let your baby begin many of the conversations. By copying the sounds your baby made, you encouraged her interest in talking and her development of a repertoire of sounds. Now, at six months, you can take a more active role in initiating conversation. Play some naming games with your baby, like naming eyes, nose, hands, and toys.

Invite a Friend

Invite a baby over to play with your baby. As babies look at, poke at and investigate each other, they are making important comparisons between toys and real people.

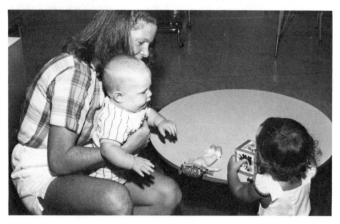

Playtime

Making Discoveries:

Play Pat-a-Cake

Play pat-a-cake with the baby over and over again.

Pat-a-cake, pat-a-cake Baker's man
Bake me a cake as fast as you can
Roll it, and knead it, and mark it with a "B"
And put it in the oven for Baby and me.

Cup Talk

Gather several empty cups in a variety of sizes. Place them in a shoe box. Talk into one cup at a time repeating a familiar sound (e.g. your child's name). Baby will notice how unusual her name sounds coming out of different cups. Now, don't stop— make a variety of noises and sounds. The more you demonstrate, the more your baby will imitate.

Water Balloons

Fill up a small balloon with a 1/4 cup of water. Tie a knot in the balloon. Show your baby how it changes shape as you squeeze and wiggle it! Now for the fun—let the baby experiment. She'll soon discover it will bounce when you drop it and wiggle when you roll it. Be with the baby at all times. Remember, a broken balloon can be dangerous if baby puts it in her mouth.

Play a Sound Game

Fill plastic bottles with different amounts of water. Tap the bottles with a spoon to produce different sounds. The baby will notice the differences in sound. After a while she will join in the game.

Pin Up a Mom and Dad Photo

Name Mommy and Daddy at every opportunity. Place a large picture of Mommy and Daddy near the baby's crib or high chair. When baby babbles "ma-ma" or "da-da", answer her by pointing to the picture on the wall and say, "There is Mommy (or Daddy)."

Developing Coordination:

Play "Pop Goes the Weasel"

Play pop-goes-the-weasel with the baby. Say the rhyme slowly. When you reach the "pop," raise the baby's arms high in the air. She will learn to anticipate the "pop" and will laugh when you reach the last line. (Be careful not to swing your baby by the arms or pull her arms out with a jerk. The baby's arms can be dislocated easily.)

Play a Piggy-Back Game

Let the baby ride "piggy-back" on Daddy's shoulders. This helps the baby develop balance and control and gives her a chance to look at the world from a different perspective.

Give the Baby a Foot Ride

While sitting on a comfortable chair, give baby an old-fashioned pony ride on your leg. Cross your legs and put baby on your ankle. Hold her hands or place your hand under her arms. Lift your leg up and down as you sing:

This is the way Amanda rides, Amanda rides, Amanda rides (ride slowly)
This is the way Amanda rides so early in the morning.
Repeat using "cowboys"—and give baby a faster ride.

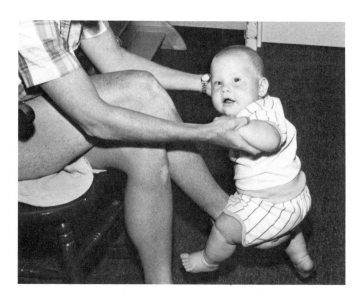

If Baby Has Started to Crawl

Make a simple obstacle course of different textured pillows for the baby to crawl across.

Roll and Crawl

Using a flutter ball is an excellent method for encouraging baby to crawl. Roll it slowly away from your baby. Verbally direct baby's attention to the ball. "Go get the ball—hurry-get the ball."

Ball Play

Put the baby in a sitting position. Roll the ball back and forth, singing:

I roll the ball to Baby
She rolls it back to me.

Solving Problems:

Hand Baby Three Toys

Hand the baby a third toy when she has a toy in each hand. At first she will try to grasp the third toy with her hands full. But with lots of practice she will learn how to put one toy down before she grasps for a new one.

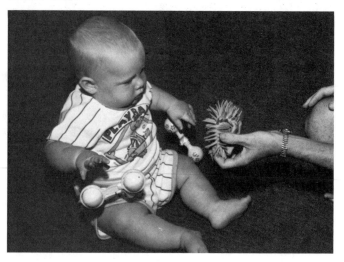

Half-Hide a Toy Under a Blanket

Partially hide a favorite toy under a blanket or square of material. Your baby will learn to pull at the part of the toy she sees. Eventually, she will learn to remove the blanket.

Slide a Doll Across the Table

Slide a rag doll across a table so that your baby can watch it fall off. After a while she will anticipate the fall and look down on the floor before the doll falls off.

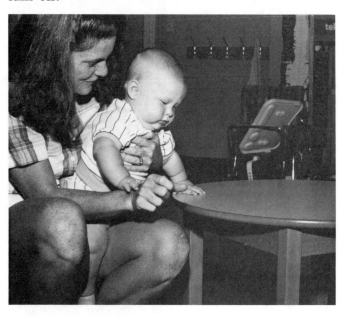

Pie Tin Fun

Give the baby two pie tins. Show her how to bang them together or bang them on the table.

Hide a Wind-Up Radio

Hide a wind-up radio under a diaper and see if you baby can retrieve it.

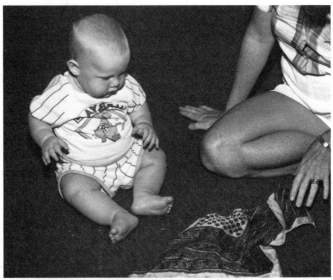

Tie a Helium Balloon to Baby's Stroller

Baby will enjoy watching the balloon and pulling down on the string to make the balloon move. (Do not leave your baby alone with the balloon. If it bursts she may try to mouth it.)

**Put Up a Busy
Board**

This is a good age to introduce your baby to a busy board. Choose one that has several items easy enough for small hands. Make sure the board is placed where it is accessible to your baby during playtime.

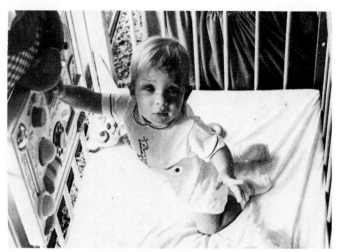

Wave Bye-Bye

Waving bye-bye when you leave the room for a moment or two is a way to prepare your baby for long departures.

Daily Routines

Mealtime:

**Use a High Chair
or Baby Chair
for Feeding**

Six months is an age when many babies are able to sit comfortably in a high chair or baby chair. Help baby develop her finger dexterity by giving her small bits of food to pick up. For starters, try Cheerios or bits of unsalted crackers.

Attach a Suction Cup Toy to the High Chair

There are a number of nice toys available that stick to the baby's tray. This will keep her busy while she is waiting for her dinner.

Help Baby Imitate Banging

When baby begins to bang on the high chair try taking a turn and see if you can get a back-and-forth game going. Emphasize the word *bang* so baby can learn to associate a word with an activity.

Mello Jello

Let baby experiment with texture by introducing her to mello jello. Make small firm blocks of jello by using plain Knox gelatin and juices. Baby will love to catch the jello as it squirms around on her tray.

Straws

If you're eating at a fast food restaurant, use the straws and lids from drinking cups as an instant toy. Thread several lids on the straw—leaving some space between them. Show the baby how to pull the lids off.

Quiet Time:

Make Happy-Sad Pillow

Make the baby a happy-sad pillow. Show her one side and then the other. This will help baby notice the differences in facial expressions. When she shows interest in the two sides of the pillow, let her play with her happy-sad plate puppet.

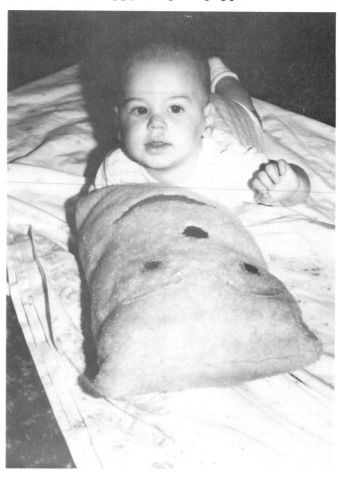

Give Baby Large Rag Doll

Give the baby a large rag doll and allow her to move the arms and legs up and down. Using short sentences, talk to the baby about what she is doing.

SEVEN MONTHS

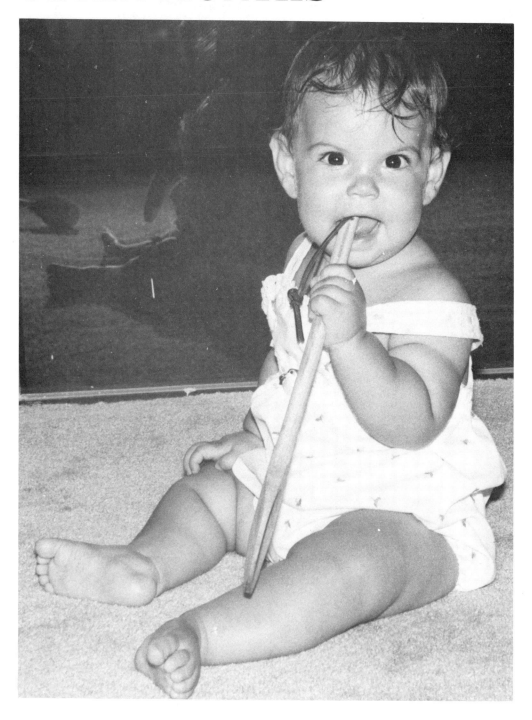

Baby's Viewpoint: Whether he's sitting in the middle of the floor or crawling around, the seven month old baby is expanding his territory. At one moment he will pick up a set of keys and, in a manner of speaking, put them through their paces, shaking, banging, and waving them in the air, transferring them from one hand to the other, shoving them into his mouth. The next moment he picks up another toy and repeats the same routine. If someone approaches him during this play, he will look up for a minute or two and then return to his game.

Your baby's extended investigation of an object and his ability to return to an activity after an interruption are evidence of an increased capacity to plan ahead and to hold an image in memory. At the same time, this behavior foreshadows a new level of problem solving. As your baby plays with different objects and examines and compares their properties, he makes the intuitive discovery that he can handle more than one object at a time. His thinking skills are expanding to match his widening field of exploration.

Motor Skills

Most babies are able to sit alone at seven months old. They no longer need their hands for balance and can use them to reach, grasp, bang, shake and poke. Crawling, too, is often achieved by this age. An active seven month old baby may take the next step and pull himself up to a standing position. Getting back down, of course, is another story. It is not unusual for a baby to pull up to a standing position, and then cry in panic until someone comes to pull him back down again. As these motor skills emerge, a baby's sleep may be disturbed. Even a good sleeper will awaken himself by trying to crawl or stand up in his sleep. It is as if the baby can't waste time sleeping with such important new skills to practice.

The seven month old baby is also busy practicing his ability to handle objects. Usually the baby does not demonstrate a strong hand preference. He will play with a toy first with one hand and then with the other, with one hand mirroring what the other hand has just done. Even if a baby clearly uses one hand more often than the other, it doesn't mean that he is right-handed or left-handed. He may change preferred hands several times before he makes a permanent choice.

Seeing, Hearing, and Feeling

One of the most striking characteristics of the seven month old is his interest in visual detail. He immediately notices the pattern on a new sheet and will scratch the design with his fingers as if trying to pick it up. He is also becoming interested in the relationship of one object to another. He picks a block up in one hand, examines it with his eyes, picks up another block in the other hand, puts it through the same kind of examination and then bangs the two together.

The seven month old baby investigates the orientation of objects in space. Your baby can now recognize a familiar object like a bottle or teddy bear when it is upside down and is quite likely to turn it over. Curious about his own orientation in space, he squirms and wiggles in his mother's arms, then throws back his head to see what things look like upside down.

The seven month old is beginning to realize that one object can be on top of another, even if it looks like the two objects are one. For example, if a small object like a poker chip is placed on a larger object of similar shape, like a saucer, the baby may see that the poker chip can be picked up without disturbing the saucer.

Baby may investigate the spatial relationship of front and back. Flat objects, such as books and pan lids, will be flipped from front to back over and over again as the baby tries to figure out how these two different looking sides can be part of the same object. Round objects, which have no sides, are the most surprising of all. The baby may rotate a round object several times as if trying to discover some sign of a corner, some indication that there is a front and back, or a top and bottom.

In the process of investigating objects, baby discovers that some toys have moving parts and that other toys change shape. This intrigues him. He will catch hold of a string on a toy or the label of a stuffed toy—and swing the toy around. He will spend as long as ten minutes crumpling a piece of aluminum foil.

When the six month old baby searched for a rattle that was partly hidden under his blanket, he showed some understanding of object permanence. Now, at seven months, he has developed still another insight into the nature of objects. When baby drops a toy off his feeding table, he looks down on the floor to see where it is. Remember, just a few months ago he continued to look in the place where he saw it last as if his looking could make it reappear. By looking to see where his toy has landed, baby demonstrates his growing understanding that, when a rattle drops, it will fall to the floor and remain there.

Another sign of increased understanding is baby's ability to go back to an activity that has been briefly interrupted. For example, baby may be banging two blocks together when you enter the room. He'll stop and look at you for a moment and then go back to his banging. The baby remembers his blocks are there, despite the momentary distraction.

The baby's understanding of hidden objects is also apparent in a game of peek-a-boo. Peek-a-boo is a top favorite for the seven to eight month old baby, and it helps the baby learn that objects which disappear from sight are not necessarily gone forever. When Mother reappears from underneath a scarf, the baby's delighted laugh signals both his enjoyment of the game and his sense of relief. Although he guessed it all along, it's nice to know for sure that Mother is really still there.

Knowing Your Baby

Baby's own vocabulary of sounds is increasing on a daily basis. Interestingly enough, many of the vowel sounds that he was practicing at two and three months old have been dropped. He is more likely now to practice a string of consonants. Often a baby discovers one particular babble and practices it for a week or so before going on to a new one.

Baby enjoys listening to Mommy and Daddy talk and may be content to play alone for an hour or more if they talk to him from time to time. A real forward step is baby's ability to recognize his own name. He demonstrates this new learning by interrupting his play and looking toward the person calling his name. Your baby is also learning to use gestures to control the people around him. If he wants his Dad to continue playing a game with him, he may yank at his Daddy's arm or bounce impatiently up and down. When he notices something interesting across the room and wants to share his discovery, he may point his hand in that direction and wiggle with excitement.

With familiar adults, the seven month old baby delights in using objects to play a back and forth social game. He hands a toy to Daddy, then puts out his hand to get it back. He finds a toy that is hidden in Mother's hand and returns it to her hand in order to replay the game. The baby is creating a game with toys that parallels earlier parent-child "conversations." He may even engage in such a game with a stranger, as long as the newcomer lets the baby do the approaching.

Despite this willingness to make new friends, baby continues to be wary of strangers. He not only objects to the sudden appearance of a new face, but even when the stranger stays around for a while, his shy behavior may persist. Along with the baby's increased ability to recognize an unfamiliar face comes a new sensitivity to changes in facial expression or tone of voice. When an adult tells the baby "no" in a sharp voice, the baby stops what he is doing, at least for a couple of seconds.

SUGGESTED ACTIVITIES
Setting the Stage

Let Baby Watch Children at Play

Baby loves to watch other children at play. Give him opportunities to play with older children and to have a friend his own age over for a visit.

Introduce Your Baby to Records

Babies respond differently to different kinds of music. Watch how your baby responds. Does he move in rhythm to records with a strong beat, and relax and get sleepy with others?

Arrange Toys so Baby Can Stand Up and Play

Babies enjoy sitting or standing in different positions when they play with toys. If your baby is learning to stand, take the breakable ornaments off the coffee table and line up his favorite toys.

Name Toys for Baby

Give the baby toys to play with that can be named easily: cup, telephone, doll, kitten, spoon, dog, block, rattle, banana, clown.

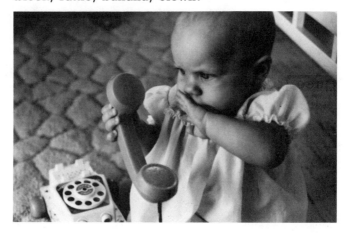

Playtime

Making Discoveries:

**Show Your
Baby Pictures**

Cut out large pictures from magazines—a telephone, a dog, an airplane, a spoon, a teddy bear. Paste the pictures over the pages of a pamphlet you were going to toss out. Now sit your baby on your lap and "read" about the pictures.

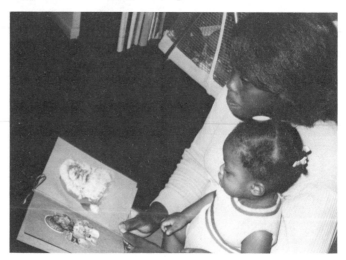

**Show Baby a
Doll in the
Mirror**

Help baby explore mirror images. Show him a rag doll and then encourage him to look at the doll in the mirror. Watch to see if baby looks back and forth between the real doll and his image.

**Give Baby Toys
That Talk Back**

Your baby is discovering in more and more ways that he can make things happen. Look for toys that "react" to your baby's manipulations, like Busy Boxes, squeak toys, pull toys, and pop-up toys.

Coffee Can Drop

Now that your baby has mastered the skill of sitting, he can sit on the floor to play some dropping games. Dropping a hard ball into a coffee can is a good activity to begin with. (File rough edges on the rim of the can.) Hold your baby's hand over the coffee can and encourage him to drop the ball. He will be intrigued by the sound of the ball bouncing in the can and will want to try again. After a while he will drop the ball with just a little help.

Improving Coordination:

Balance on a Stool

Now that baby is a confident sitter, let's challenge him with a low stool. Hang or hold up an interesting toy in front of him while he is sitting on the stool.

Your baby will learn after a while how to maintain his balance while he is reaching for a toy.

**Play See-Saw
With Baby**

See-saw, up and down, Baby is going to Baby's town.
See-saw, side to side, Baby is going for a ride.
See-saw, bumpty-bump, Baby is getting ready to jump.

Your baby will listen to your inflections and will laugh out loud on the last line in anticipation of the "jump."

Punch Ball Fun

Hang a punch ball from the ceiling. Baby will enjoy batting at it and watching it dance about.

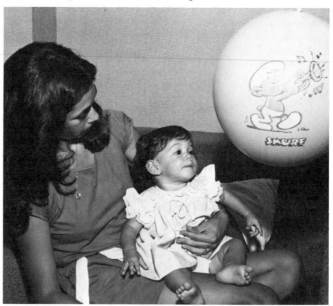

Tug of War

Have a tug of war with baby. Give him one end of a scarf, pull gently on the other end. Your baby will enjoy this playful lesson in turn taking.

Solving Problems:

Attach a Ribbon to a Toy

Attach a ribbon to the head of a small rag doll or clown. Show the baby how to hold the clown up by the ribbon in order to make him dance.

Give Baby Several Small Balls

Give the baby several small rubber balls to pick up. Now that the baby is developing the ability to use his thumb independently, he needs opportunities to practice.

Bang Two Toys Together

Bang two toys together. Then let the baby try it.

Hide a Squeak Toy

Make one of the baby's toys squeak, then hide it under a blanket while the baby is watching you. Let him try to find it.

Hide and Seek— Which Hand?

Place a small interesting toy in the palm of your hand. Let your baby see it—just for a moment—and then close your hand. Encourage baby to find the hidden object. Your baby will learn that objects do not disappear forever when they are out of sight. Clap with enthusiasm when baby discovers the toy. Play the game several times. If baby has difficulty discovering the toy by himself, show it to him again.

Daily Routines

Bathtime

Floating Toys

Put several different floating toys in the baby's bath. Each time he retrieves one, examine it with him and talk about it.

Let Baby Do the "Back Stroke"

Fill the bath tub with only 2"-3" of water. Lay the baby on his back and watch how much kicking he does.

Save a Special Toy for Diapering

If your baby has started to squirm away at every diaper change, keep a special toy on the changing table to hand him as a distractor.

Sing "This is the Way"

While bathing or diapering baby sing to the tune of "Here We Go Round The Mulberry Bush:"

This is the way we wash our toes, wash our toes, wash our toes,
This is the way we wash our toes
So early in the morning.

Repeat, singing: wash our face, change our diaper, kiss baby's tummy, say hello, etc.

Bath Cup

If your baby seems to spill more than drink, why not provide him with an appropriate practice space—the tub. He can fill, spill, and drink—and no worry or mess.

Mealtime:

Let Baby Hand Feed

Give the baby some food with every meal that he can pick up with his fingers such as diced carrots, peas, bits of hamburger, or bits of unprocessed cheese.

Let Baby Finger Paint

Put a dab of plain yogurt on your baby's tray and let him paint with his fingers.

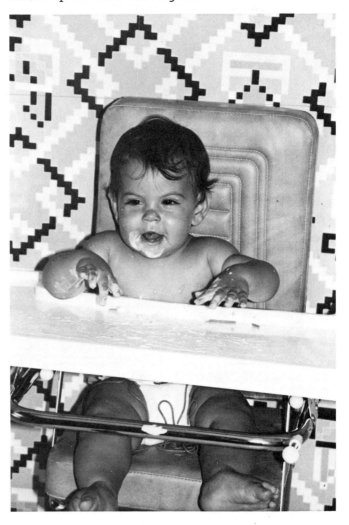

Give Baby Some Spaghetti

Pulling apart strands of spaghetti is a challenging game.

Self-Help

Try letting your baby hold his own bottle but, if he objects, give up the idea. Some babies are not ready for quite this much independence.

Quiet Time:

Reading With Baby

This is a good age to begin reading real books. Choose a baby book with sturdy pages and very vivid pictures (cloth books are more indestructible but the pictures are not as bright). Sit baby comfortably on your lap. As you turn the pages, name the picture and talk about it. "Look at baby—See the baby. Ooh—touch the baby." End the activity before your baby gets squirmy. You want your baby to associate reading with being happy, comfortable and encircled with love.

Show Baby the Light Switch— Show Baby the Light

Before you turn off the light, say, "Light's out." After a while your baby will make the connection.

EIGHT MONTHS

Baby's Viewpoint: The eight month old baby is, in a way, a kind of enigma. On the one hand, she is becoming an adventuresome explorer, creeping away from her parents to investigate new territories. On the other hand, she is a timid soul shying away from strangers, afraid of new places and resistant to going to sleep in an unfamiliar crib.

Actually, both baby's increased adventuresomeness and her timidity are related to increased awareness. As the baby's memory span increases she is able to distinguish between situations that are new and situations that are familiar. She knows that a foray into the new room is safe because she can keep in mind both the image of her mother's face and the route back.

A new person, a new face, or a new bed is quite a different story. She cannot attach the new experience to anything familiar and cannot make a prediction as to what will happen next. All she knows is that the new person is not Mommy or Daddy, the new place has no familiar landmarks, and the new bed is not a place that's warm and safe for sleeping. She expresses her dismay with a scream and if mother arrives to find out what's wrong, she buries her head in the safety of mother's arm.

Motor Skills

A new accomplishment for many eight month old babies is the ability to climb up stairs. Once the baby has mastered the first couple of stairs the next ones are easier. Enthusiasm takes over and up the baby goes to the top of the stairs. Getting back down the stairs is quite another matter. Hopefully, Mother is at hand to get her out of the predicament.

Parents solve the stair problem in many ways. Despite the inconvenience to other family members, the most common solution is a set of gates. Other parents are concerned about gates being left open accidentally and prefer to teach their baby a safe way to get back down the stairs. Of course, no solution is fool-proof and parents recognize that their baby's only real safeguard is a watchful adult.

Even if there are no stairs to worry about, the parent of an active eight month old must maintain a constant vigil. The baby who is trying to pull up and stand may pull on lamp cords, plant stands, virtually anything she can reach. Pieces of furniture that tip are particularly dangerous. The baby has little knowledge of stability.

The baby at eight months is quite adept at using her thumb and forefinger to pick up small bits of food. Because she can move around and get into new places, it is particularly important to keep beads, buttons and other small objects away from baby. Things that get picked up are still quite likely to find their way to baby's mouth.

The eight month old baby demonstrates her knowledge of a familiar environment by navigating through it. As she creeps around the house, she finds her way around tables and chairs, backs out of closets, and ducks her head when she finds herself under a low bed. To some degree she can tell the difference between a spot that is safe and a spot that is dangerous and is not too likely to fall off the end of a bed, or roll off the changing table. Of course, the very fact that the baby is careful most of the time makes it doubly important for parents to stay on their guard.

Seeing, Hearing, and Feeling

At seven months old your baby was especially attracted to toys that had labels, handles, strings, or any "grabable" parts. Although this interest continues at eight months, the baby's fascination is with toys that either come apart or somehow fit into each other. She is just becoming aware of containers and is delighted by her daily discoveries of new kinds of containers—pots with dirt, dog dishes with water, mouths with teeth, boxes with tissues, and purses full of all kinds of delightful things. Now her greatest joy is in emptying containers—within a month she will develop an interest in putting things inside each other.

As baby empties containers and investigates their contents, she is continuing her self study on the properties of objects. One of the major concepts that your baby is grappling with is the idea that objects exist even when you can't see them. With actions rather than words your baby keeps asking the question, "Will the set of keys that just fell into a plastic bucket still be there when I reach inside?" By the age of eight months she can solve the mystery of a disappearing object—if the object is hidden in an obvious way. A teddy bear that is covered with a blanket can be uncovered, a toy that disappears into Dad's shirt pocket can be fished out. Each of these experiences provides insight into object permanence.

Baby's best way to learn about object permanence, however, is to watch her parents leave and return. Because of the baby's special attachment to her parents she pays particular attention to their comings and goings. She notices when Mommy or Daddy leaves in the morning and watches out the window when Mommy or Daddy comes home. She learns all the signs of her parents' coming and going. She knows, for example, that if Mommy puts on her hat and coat, or Daddy puts the leash on the dog, they are about to go outside.

When baby is inside the house she is likely to expend a great deal of energy keeping track of her parents. Despite her efforts to keep them in view, parents are continually going in and out of the room, answering the telephone, turning off the washing machine, or attending to other household chores. The eight month old may call out anxiously when a parent leaves the room, but gradually she learns that as long as she can hear a familiar voice her parent is still home. A baby who has mastered creeping can even begin venturing into another room on her own, then returning a few seconds later to check back with Mommy and Daddy. As baby discovers her own ability to leave and come back, she recognizes more and more clearly that people and objects continue to exist when they are out of her sight.

Peek-a-boo and hide and seek games which are related to the baby's discovery of object permanence continue to be charged with excitement. In a favorite version of peek-a-boo, Mother hides her head under the blanket and baby shrieks with delight as she pulls the blanket away. It is as if the baby is saying, "Look what I just did. I made my disappeared Mommy come back."

Everyday, in the course of her active investigations, the eight month old comes across new questions to ask and new problems to solve. She hears an airplane sound and looks up in the sky. She tries to touch the sound in a wound-up music box. She wonders how she can reach the goldfish when her hand won't go through the glass. What will happen if she pulls on the string of a pull toy, her big sister's hair, or the corner of the cloth on the dining room table?

Knowing Your Baby

At eight months, baby's babbling includes almost all the sounds of her language. Talking on a toy telephone is apt to be a favorite game. Some babies prefer the real telephone, while others seem frightened when a familiar voice that usually comes from Daddy's mouth is all of a sudden inside the phone.

Although the eight month old has not mastered meaningful words, she is quite adept at using babble messages to communicate her intentions. "Dadada" is likely to be an invitation to play—a whiny "mamama" may mean, "I need some cuddling," and a high pitched string of vowels may mean, "Don't you go out of this room, I want you here." The eight month old is also sensitive to tone of voice. Without knowing what you are saying she knows full well when you are pleased, excited, cross, or indifferent.

Handing a toy back and forth is still a fun way to play with adults, but now some new object games are appearing. Baby enjoys a game of ball according to her own rules. She will retrieve the ball that you throw across the room and expect you to retrieve the ball that she tosses. Another version of the game involves sweeping all the toys off the high chair and watching Mommy pick them up. Mothers, of course, get tired of the game long before babies.

The eight month old is receptive to imitative games. Mother and baby may take turns patting a squeak doll, banging a pot, drinking from a cup, putting a hat on their head. Now baby may be able to imitate an activity even when she can't see the part of her that is doing the imitating. This new skill is associated both with her improved visual memory and her developing recognition that things can still be there even when she doesn't see them.

SUGGESTED ACTIVITIES

Setting the Stage

Now that baby is "on the go" and can explore many parts of the house, make her world interesting (and safe!). Give the baby her own cabinet in the kitchen filled with containers and spoons. A special drawer in the bathroom will keep baby busy as Mom and Dad get ready to go out. Fill the drawer with rollers, interesting boxes, books, or toys. Small baskets of toys kept in different rooms give the baby something new and exciting to play with as she moves through the house.

Talk to Baby in Short But Complete Sentences

Carry on a running commentary about things you and baby are doing.

Build Up Your Baby's Library

There are a number of books that babies love at this age. Activity books such as "Pat the Bunny" and "Telephone" are particularly enjoyed. Let the baby read a variety of books: books with one picture on each page so she can learn new words, books with more detailed pictures so she can search for a special friend or favorite object, and books with short rhymes to accompany the pictures.

Playtime

Making Discoveries:

Visit! Visit! Visit!

Baby is very aware of other people at this age. She loves talking to both grown ups and children. It is also an age where some babies become fearful of strangers. Help your baby through this time by giving her as many opportunities as possible to be around other people.

Telephone Games

Encourage your baby to talk. Let her play with a toy phone or, better yet, unplug yours and give her the real thing.

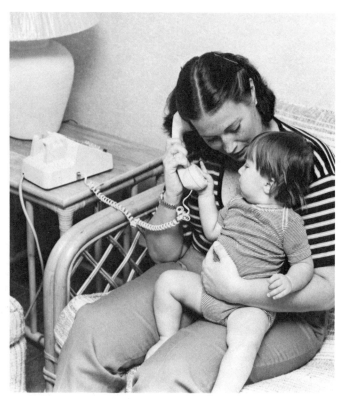

**Call Attention
to Sounds**

Call the baby's attention to different sounds by naming the source of the sound: the telephone, door bell, Daddy's footsteps, rain, running water, dog barking. As the baby pays attention to sounds, she is learning the habit of listening—important for development of speech.

**Talk About
Outdoor Noises**

Take the baby outside in a carriage or stroller. When you see a bird, hear an airplane, or notice a dog approach, share your baby's excitement. Pointing with your finger say, "Airplane, airplane, see the airplane." Your baby will learn to look in the direction of your pointing and will associate words with exciting objects that move.

**Play a Hat
Game With Baby**

Give the baby a "hat" that she can put on her head. As she tries to find her head, she is learning more about herself. Try the game with different kinds of hats, or even a bowl. Let the baby admire herself in the mirror.

More Language

Babies are drawn to animals. Get baby a set of plastic animals and show her the noise each one makes. "The dog says woof, woof. Can you find the dog?"

Pie Tin With Oatmeal

When baby is sitting out in the grass, put oatmeal in a pie tin. She will enjoy mixing it with her hand or feeling the oatmeal slide through her fingers.

Improving Coordination:

Play Row-Row-Row Your Boat

Do situps with baby as you sing, "Row-row-row your boat, gently down the stream; merrily, merrily, merrily, merrily, life is but a dream." Vary the pace. Sing the song fast and then slow, loud and then soft, sway baby to the side as well as up and down.

Wheelbarrow Walk

With your baby lying on her stomach, lift her legs two or three inches from the floor. While she supports herself on her arms, encourage her to "walk" forward.

Playing Hiding Games With Baby

Crawling babies love hiding and chase games. Hide behind a chair and call to baby so she can find you. Give baby a turn to hide.

Crawling Over, Under, and Through

As baby is creeping and cruising and eventually walking she is discovering some new facts about the size of her body and the objects in her world. What will she fit under? What can she crawl over? How far can she reach? The more experience of this kind she has, the more she becomes aware of the size of her body and the amount of space her body takes up. You can provide baby with some of these experiences by encouraging her to crawl through a tunnel, under a table, or over a mound of pillows.

Swing Baby

Swing the baby in your arms or on a swing, or ride her up and down on your knee. These games help the baby develop balance and control.

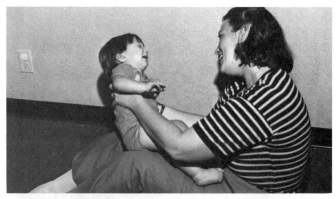

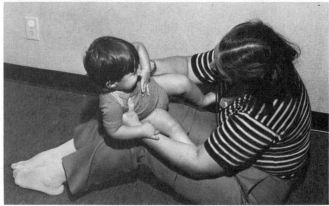

Climb and Fetch

If stairs are available, use them to help baby exercise. Place a toy at a higher stair than baby. Climbing up the stairs is a task most babies thoroughly enjoy. It is better to teach her how than to try to keep her from climbing. After the work of the climb, she will welcome that toy. Remember, though, baby *always* needs supervision on stairs.

Solving Problems: ˙

Play Follow the Leader

Play "follow the leader" games with the baby. Bang a drum, knock, clap your hands, wave, blow, lead an orchestra.

Banging With a Tool

Give the baby a wooden spoon and show her how to bang. Give her different surfaces to bang, a flat cookie pan, a place mat, a magazine. Your baby will enjoy the banging and will recognize differences in sound and feel.

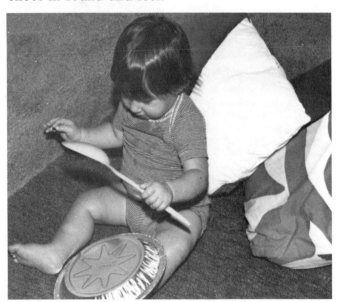

Let Baby Knock Down a Block Tower

Build a tower of blocks for baby. Show her how to knock it down. As the tower crashes use words such as, "Uh oh, it all fell down." Baby will soon delight in her ability to produce such an outstanding effect.

Turn a Cup Upside Down

Place a cup with a handle upside down on a table. See if the baby can grasp the handle and turn the cup upright. If she accomplishes this task she has learned something about the orientation of objects.

Place a Toy on a Blanket

When baby is in the highchair, place a toy on a place mat out of the baby's reach. Your baby will have to pull the mat in order to retrieve the toy. Baby's ability to accomplish this game signals a new understanding of object relationships. Your baby recognizes that one object can rest on another. If you hold the toy a little above the place mat and the baby still pulls it, you know she has not quite mastered the concept.

Hide a Toy Under a Blanket

Hide a toy under a blanket while the baby is watching. Let her lift up the blanket and find her toy. Because the baby is just learning that objects can be present even though they are covered up, there is an element of surprise in this game that adds to the fun of playing it.

Pots and Pans

Pots and pans are more fun than any store-bought toy, particularly if they are shiny. Show the baby how to put a lid on a pan (her first puzzle). As she gets more accomplished, give her two different sized pans and their lids and see if she can figure out which lid goes with each pot. It's also fun to hide things in the pots and let the baby take off the lids to find her "surprise." If you don't mind a little noise show the baby how to bang the lids together.

Make a Toy Box

Using a large cardboard box to store baby's toys is not only useful but it may provide an interesting challenge. Cut a large shape out of each side. Cover with interesting contact paper. Place baby's toys inside—now let her think how to get them out. Each toy is a different shape and will require your baby to solve a new problem.

Balls in a Bowl

A large bowl with a rounded bottom provides your baby with a new challenge. She must hold the bowl with one hand and place the balls in the bowl with the other hand. The unstable bottom makes the activity more fun.

Muffin Tins

A muffin pan game is a first experience in learning number concepts. Using a six cup muffin tin, place a tennis ball into each cup. Give the baby a turn taking them out and putting them back in.

Transparent Vs. Opaque Barriers

Now that your baby is learning about hiding games, play games where you hide a toy behind a barrier. Put a toy behind a lucite tray or picture frame. Will your baby reach for the toy directly or will she reach around to get the toy?

Cheerio Spill

Place some Cheerios in a plastic bottle. See if your baby can figure out how to tip over the bottle to feed herself some Cheerios.

Find the Picture

Put an interesting picture on one side of a carton. See if your baby will crawl around the carton until she discovers the picture.

Easter Egg Game

Place plastic Easter eggs in an egg carton. As the baby moves them about she will be giving herself an early lesson in arithmetic.

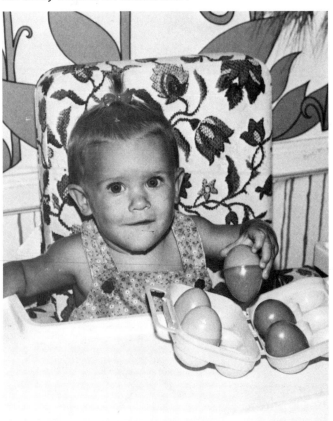

Daily Routines

Mealtime:

For Teething Baby

Make baby her own popsicles out of juice. (Tupperware has popsicle-making sets with plastic handles.) Baby will enjoy licking her popsicle and helping you hold the stick. A frozen banana works well with some babies.

**Rolling a Car
Along**

Keep your baby busy while you sit in a restaurant by showing her how to roll a small car across the tray of her high chair.

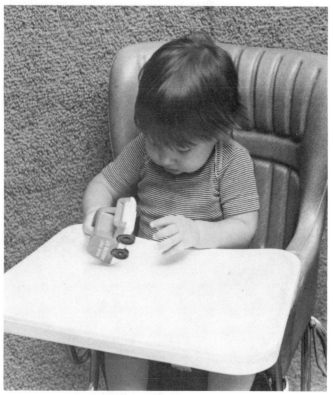

**Bathtime
Diaper Time:**

**Sing to Baby
During Bath
Time**

Sing this silly song or make up one of your own (to the tune of Twinkle Twinkle Little Star):

Twinkle twinkle little eyes
You're so little and so wise
Wash your ears and wash your nose
Washing you from tip to toes
Twinkle twinkle baby mine
Now you're scrubbed up clean and fine.

**Put Butter
Boats in Bath**

Make your own bath toy by using butter tubs for boats and placing a red rubber ball inside. Initially, baby will enjoy watching the ball in its boat. Before long she will be attempting to catch it.

Toe Hunt

Tie a bright ribbon to your baby's toe. She will have fun trying to pull it off.

Self-Help

Give your baby her own wash cloth. After a while she will make some beginning attempts to wash parts of her body.

Quiet Time:

Make Baby Some "Pat" Pictures

Make "pat" pictures using different materials and textures. Pussy willows, satins, rubber carpet ends all produce interesting sensations. "Read" with baby before she falls asleep.

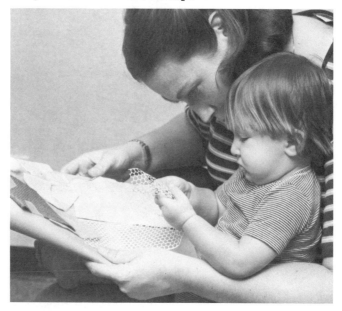

Body Parts

Make a large picture of a baby on a sheet of cardboard. Sew or securely glue pieces of fabric over individual body parts -hands, head, shoulders, toes, knees or tummy. Now play a new game of peek-a-boo. Label the parts of the doll as baby lifts up the fabric curtain. As baby begins to recognize the parts of the body, she can play the game herself.

**Place Baby in
Front of the
Window**

Hold your baby near the window in the evening. Looking out at the darkness has a calming effect.

NINE MONTHS

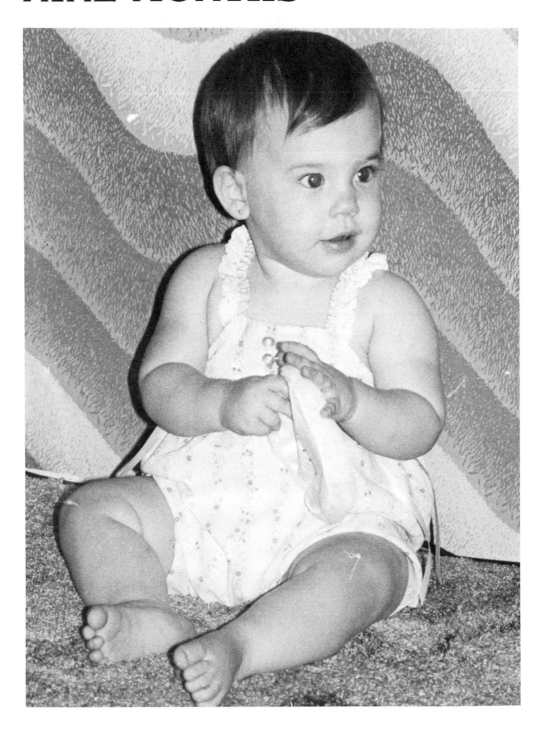

Baby's Viewpoint: As babies progress through the first year of life, individual differences both in the pace of development and in leading skills make it increasingly difficult to state precisely at what specific age a developmental milestone occurs. Remember, when we talk about the nine month old we are really talking about many, but not all, nine month olds. The one constant is the sequence of development within a particular domain. A baby, for instance, will learn to stand before he walks or to scoop an object into his hand before he picks it up with thumb and finger.

Regardless of developmental status, your nine month old baby is likely to show an interesting change in the pace of his activity. Whether he is practicing his ability to get around the house, or playing with toys, his rate of exploration is speeding up. Day by day he becomes noticeably more vigorous and his skills more proficient. At around nine months old, your baby also demonstrates a better memory for past events and an increased ability to solve simple problems. If you try to give him a spoonful of baby food that he rejected the first time, he will push it forcefully away. If you slip a toy inside his sweater he will pull up the sweater and let it fall out. Quite obviously, he is reaching a point where he can direct his efforts toward a well defined goal.

Motor Skills

By nine months old most babies have a well developed style of creeping. Hands and knees creeping, which allows babies to climb over obstacles and maneuver on different surfaces, is certainly the most common. Some babies, however, will slide along on their rear ends, some will hop forward using one leg as a pusher, some will pull themselves along the floor with their arms. Still others will creep straight kneed like a wobbly colt.

While many babies at nine months are developing new motor skills — standing, cruising, climbing up stairs, sliding off sofas — others seem to be at a standstill. All babies have peaks and plateaus in their development. They learn quite rapidly for awhile, and then need time to practice and consolidate before going on to new things. Often, however, when the baby appears not to be progressing in one area of development, he is making important gains in another area.

Nine months is an important age for developing small muscle as well as large muscle skills. While some babies spend much of their time getting ready to walk, other babies are more intent on manipulating small objects. Spoons may take on special significance. They learn that a spoon not only serves as a drumstick, it can also be used as a tool for bringing food to your mouth. Although your baby may turn the spoon upside down before it reaches his mouth, he will grasp the idea of first putting food on the spoon and then putting the spoon in his mouth.

Seeing, Hearing, and Feeling

Many babies at nine months will search selectively for a favorite toy or blanket. A dirty teddy bear tossed in with the morning wash can start a family crisis. Despite the potential problems the "favorite toy" creates, this early object attachment is an important developmental event. It shows that the baby can make fine distinctions, (a substitute teddy is rejected forcefully) and can remember what a toy looks like even when it is out of sight.

Baby's ability to make fine discriminations is as noticeable with sounds as it is with sights. He is particularly attentive to sounds that allow him to anticipate the events of the day — the buzz of a razor meaning Daddy is awake, the closing of the refrigerator door meaning breakfast is ready, the patter on the window meaning rain.

As well as making more meaningful discriminations, your baby is becoming more adept at planning ahead. This planning ability is especially evident when he is presented with a two step problem. If his favorite truck is stuck behind another toy, he will push the obstacle aside to get the truck. If you slide a plant to the other side of the coffee table out of your baby's reach, he will cruise around the coffee table in order to touch the plant. In these situations your baby is demonstrating an ability to coordinate two actions. In effect, he is using one act as a means of accomplishing another.

The same kind of advanced planning is reflected in the way baby handles familiar objects. Just two months ago your baby was putting every object he picked up through the same set of experiments, examining, shaking, banging, mouthing, etc. Now, when your baby picks up an object, the actions he performs tend to take into account the special properties of the object. He shakes a rattle because that is what rattles are for. He puts a cup to his mouth, he crinkles a piece of foil, he rings a bell. It is as if the baby is aware of a different goal with each object and the actions he performs are a means of achieving that goal.

Emptying is another goal oriented activity that becomes more prominent at nine months. Baby places a toy in a box, tips the box over, picks up the toy and places it back in the box. We can look at this kind of repetitive activity as a version of hide and seek. Baby is investigating whether or not the toy still exists when it is hidden in the box.

Now that the baby is more sure about object permanence, "hide and seek" games appear in a whole variety of forms. If you close a toy inside your hand, he will pry it open. Baby initiates his own games, opening up the kitchen cabinets, pulling out the pots and pans, and distributing them around the house. This game of course will go on for many months.

Knowing Your Baby

At nine months old your baby shows an emerging ability to attend to and respond to words. Baby will look from one parent to the other in response to "Where's Mommy?" "Where's Daddy?" He will give Mommy a spoon in answer to a simple command, especially if Mommy communicates what she wants by holding out her hand. Baby also is more apt to understand a verbal command such as "Give Mommy the spoon" if he is looking at the spoon when Mother makes the request. Once he has achieved success with this kind of game, baby will enjoy playing it over and over again.

At the same time that your baby is attaching meaning to the words he hears, he is building up his expressive vocabulary. Although much of his babble and jargoning may be just vocal play, he is also beginning to speak some words in context. He may have learned to say "bye-bye" when he waves his hand, or "dada" when a male visitor comes to his house. The first words that he learns are not likely to be requests. They are usually labels for familiar people and pets, or words that accompany a familiar action.

Parents play an important role in this very early talking stage. When the baby's tentative attempt to say "bye-bye" makes Mom and Dad excited and attentive, baby experiences the fun of using words appropriately. When baby follows a verbal command and is rewarded with parental enthusiasm, his attentiveness and responsiveness increase.

Back and forth games continue to be popular. One of the most popular, from the point of view of the babies at least, is pulling a parent's glasses off. Almost as popular is the "I'm going to bite you" game, where the baby sticks his hand in Daddy's mouth, Daddy bites down, and baby withdraws his hand and grins victoriously. A variation of the game is "I'm going to get you" when Daddy charges at baby's tummy and baby blocks the charge.

A somewhat calmer back and forth game is "telephone." Using a toy telephone or the real phone with the plug pulled out, Mother and baby each take a turn talking into the phone. Mother makes a ringing sound, models a brief conversation, "Hello, how are you? Are you eating lunch?" Then she hands the phone to baby, saying "Have your turn." After a while the baby learns to babble into the phone before trying to put the receiver back in its cradle.

When babies have had a lot of experience with different peers, or have become very familiar with one peer, we may see the same kind of turn taking, although perhaps in a more primitive form. Your baby hands a stuffed animal to a peer, the peer shoves the animal away, and your baby repeats the offer. The fact that both babies are smiling lets you know that you are watching a turn taking game.

NINE MONTHS ACTIVITIES

Setting the Stage

The nine month old baby does not take "no" very seriously and the whole house is fair game from his point of view. Recognizing his need to explore and manipulate, it is time to take another "baby-proofing" tour of your house. Any room that your baby may be in either alone or when his parents are busy, must be gone through with a fine tooth comb. You need to think about not only what the baby can do now, but what he will be learning to do in the next month. What cabinets and drawers will he open, what lamp cords will he pull on, what ornaments will he investigate and send smashing to the floor?

As you tour your house seeking out danger spots you need to think at the same time of safe things for your baby to play with. Make sure that every room where you and your baby may spend time together has a "cache" of toys or items that can be played with. Parents often reserve one low cabinet in the kitchen, one drawer in their own bedroom and one basket in the living room for nondestructible items.

When you have time to sit down and play with your baby, make sure to give your baby a chance to initiate some games. Placing a basket of new and interesting items within your baby's reach, such as a set of keys, some film cans, some dried fruits, and some hair rollers can inspire your baby to begin a game of passing back and forth.

Playtime

Making Discoveries:

Let Baby Ring a Bell

Give the baby a bell and show him how to ring it.

Make Baby a "Feel" Game

Give the baby his own box of "feel" materials. Make sure that it includes rough materials as well as smooth ones. A good collection of feel items might include a linoleum square, a playing card, a large rubber sink stopper, a square of velvet or satin fabric, and a sponge. Cut the boarders of the fabrics with pinking shears so they won't ravel. As the baby empties and fills his feel box, he learns to distinguish different textures.

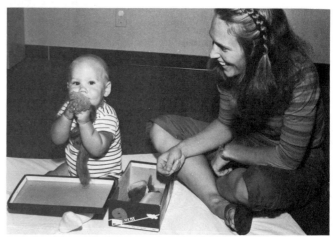

Turn Toys Upside Down

Turn toys upside down and put them in front of baby. (Teddy bear standing on his head, etc.) Encourage the baby to turn the toys right side up.

Sticky Stuff

Put a piece of scotch tape on the back of your baby's hand. Pulling it off will be an interesting challenge.

Put a Hat on Baby

Put a hat on your baby's head when he is sitting in front of a mirror. He will enjoy watching his reflection as he pulls the hat off his head.

Improving Coordination:

Play a Hand-Clapping Game

Play a hand-clapping game with your baby. Clap his hands together and then hide them under a blanket. He will love watching his hands go away and come back.

Clap your hands, one-two-three
Play a clapping game with me.
Now your hands have gone away,
Find your hands so we can play.

Roll a Ball to Baby

Roll a ball back and forth to the baby. Let the family join the game. A soft fabric ball is particularly desirable.

Sit Downs

If your baby is in that in-between stage where he can pull himself up but can't figure out how to get back down, let him practice holding on to the end of a towel or broom handle while you hold the other end. You can ease him back down to a sitting position.

Solving Problems:

Give Baby a Spindle Toy

Once he has learned to place the ring on the spindle he will practice again and again. Add an extra challenge by using a spindle that rocks.

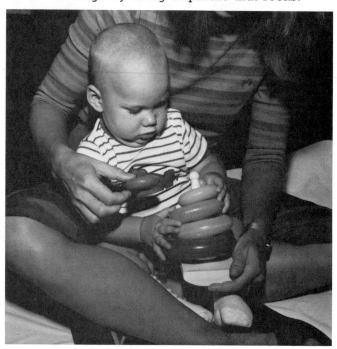

Place Toys in a See-Through Box

Put some of the baby's toys in a plastic see-through shoebox. Let the baby try to take the cover off himself. If he can't do it, take the cover half off for him.

**Upside Down
Pot**

Hand the baby a pot upside down. See if he will turn it over. Your baby is learning more and more about spatial relationships.

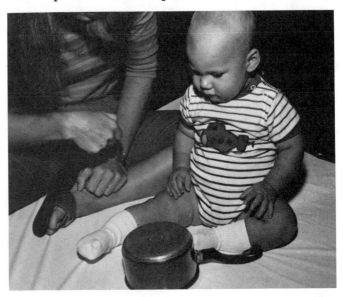

**Let Baby Drop
Toys in a Bowl**

Give the baby a pile of very large wooden beads and a plastic bowl. Show him how to drop the beads into the container. After a while the baby will learn how to reach in and get the beads.

**Play "Give Me
the Toy" Games**

Place three different toys in a box. Name one of the toys and ask the baby to hand it to you. Make a fuss over him when he gets it right.

Scarf Pull

Tie several colorful scarves together. Insert one end into a cardboard tube. Let the baby pull the scarves through the tube. Now—a new problem, can the baby stuff the scarves back into the tube?

Daily Routines

Mealtime:

Feeding Teddy

When your baby is learning to use a cup, give his teddy an occasional sip. Perhaps baby will copy what you are doing. This early game of let's pretend is a forerunner of later imaginative play.

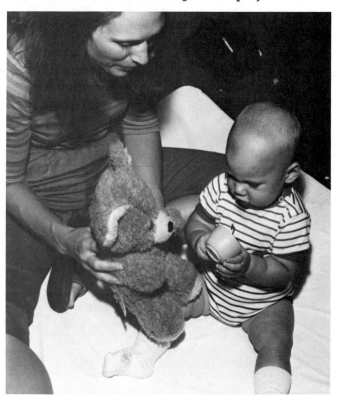

Food for Thought

Cooking is interesting for children of all ages and even a baby can be involved in preparations. Give baby a pot, lid and spoon. As you empty a box or container—give it to baby. He will enjoy imitating by holding the rice box over the pot—then stirring and banging.

Diapering Time:

Diaper Duet

Diapering is difficult at nine months. It is usually easier to catch the baby "on the run" rather than placing him on the changing table. Speed up the routine by singing a special ditty when you change his diapers.

> Zip—zip zip— off it goes
> I see baby without clothes
> Zip—zip—What do I see?
> Diaper going on with a one-two-three

Catch a Baby

Another way to meet the diapering challenge is to join in the fun! As baby tries to escape—grab his legs and pull him back—"I've got you!" Playing this several times will amuse and tire baby (long enough for you to change him at least).

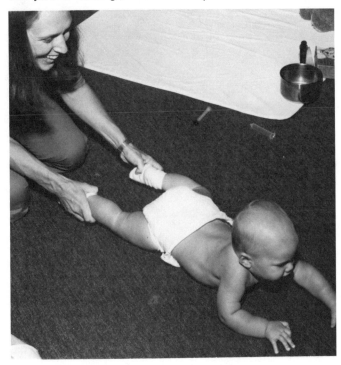

Powder Puff

While your baby is being changed he might enjoy a clean powder puff or cotton ball to explore. Show him how to rub it on his tummy, arms, nose or face. Not only will he be still for the change—you can emphasize body parts.

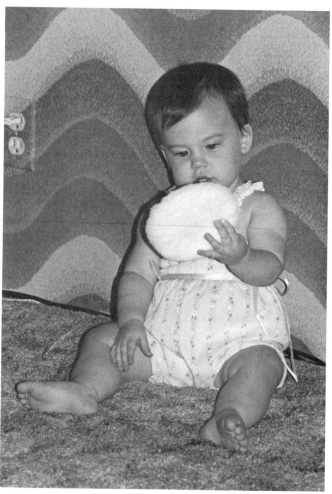

Eensy Weesny Spider

That familiar old tune becomes new if we let the "spider" walk up the baby's leg, and around his tummy. It isn't nearly as hard for baby to stay still if he is enjoying a game.

Bathtime:

**Let Baby Help
With the Bath**

Give the baby his own washcloth at bath time and his own towel for drying. Encourage the baby to help wash and dry himself. Self-help takes a lot of time and preparation.

Kick Kick

Baby loves to follow directions. Say "kick kick" in rhythm to his feet. When he stops kicking —you stop calling "kick kick!" The game will develop into a fun session of stop and go. Your baby is learning the enjoyment of language and at the same time exercising his muscles.

Quiet Time:

Share a Book

Sharing a quiet book with your baby is important at this age. Reserve time every day to read to your baby. He will appreciate the closeness. Point out the familiar pictures—cup, a ball, teddy bear, shoe, etc.

Sleep Waltz

Dance with your baby to quiet music before putting him to sleep. He has to spend much of his day exploring by himself on the floor. He needs some close cuddling before he falls asleep.

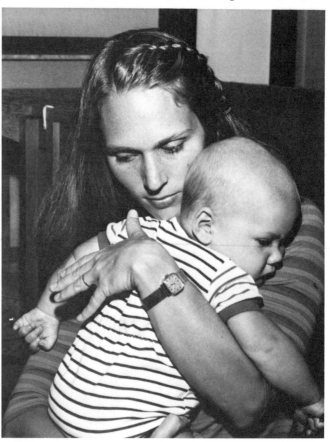

TEN MONTHS

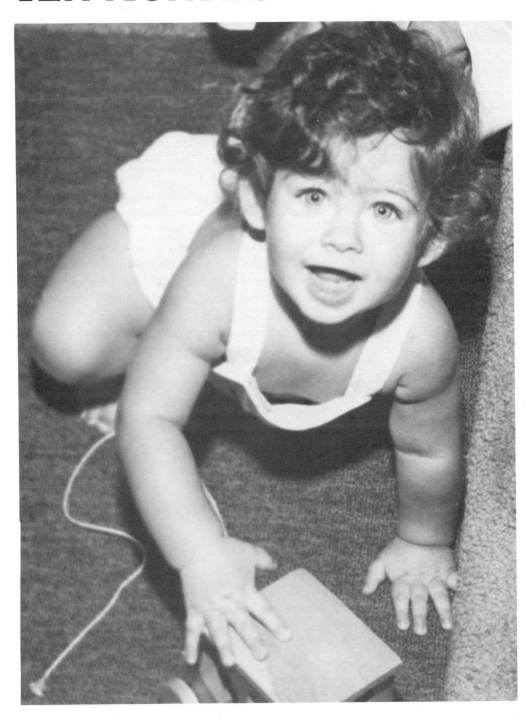

Baby's Viewpoint: Ten months is a perfect age for "baby watching." The ten month old is apt to be so busy with her own play agenda that she doesn't pay too much attention to her appreciative audience. At this age baby seems to be exploring a new question, "Can I use one object to make something happen to another object?" Of course, the baby asks this question with actions rather than words. Her experience playing with two objects at once has led naturally to the idea of using one object as a tool. Typical examples are using a spoon to chase a pea around her high chair tray, or using a strainer to bang out a "tune" on a pan.

Here again, we see the baby separating an action sequence into means and ends. The object she is using serves as the "means," while the effect she produces is the end.

As your baby becomes interested in more complicated social games, you will become aware of a change in your own way of playing, too. When your baby was under six months the games you played most often involved back and forth conversations or exercises. Your baby enjoyed these "contact" games, which often were emotionally intense and laughter producing. As your baby learned to reach for and grasp toys, these play objects became a prominent ingredient in parent-child play. Now that your baby is ten months old, contact games such as peek-a-boo, chase and singing activities still provide a feeling of excitement and intimacy. However, new toy playing and toy sharing activities seem to predominate. They offer effective ways to teach your baby while playing with her.

Motor Skills

At ten months of age individual differences in motor development are still very apparent. While one ten month old baby might just be learning to creep well, a second may already be a good walker. Despite the old adage, "You have to crawl before you walk," it isn't necessarily so. Some babies, especially if they have a close-in-age sibling, spend little or no time in the crawling stage. They devote their energies to two legged activities, pulling up on tables, chairs, or a parent's pant leg, and commanding their parents in a torrent of babbles to walk along holding their hands.

In marked contrast to the baby who is intent on walking is the baby who becomes an expert creeper. In actuality, a baby who is a proficient creeper gets around much more quickly, and is certainly better balanced, than the baby who is an early walker. She is also less likely to hurt herself when exploring a new territory. Both the creeper and the walker can go around obstacles, climb up stairs, or investigate interesting objects.

The baby who is really into creeping will show a lengthy progression of skills, at first moving hands and legs one at a time, then developing a cross pattern creep with opposite hand and foot moving together, and finally creeping so quickly and smoothly that you will have difficulty identifying the pattern. The efficient creeper also learns to creep holding an object or pushing a toy along, much as the beginning walker tries to carry or push along a toy.

Interestingly enough, there is no direct correlation between motor skills and intellectual ability. Knowing that a baby is an early walker tells us nothing about how bright the baby is, or whether she will be a good problem solver. Furthermore, independent walking cannot be rushed. Each baby has her own developmental timetable and will walk as soon as she is ready.

Most babies can pull themselves to a standing position at ten months of age. In fact, many babies will be steady enough to balance themselves without holding on to a support. Your baby may take advantage of this new stability and use her hands to pound on the support. In the morning she may greet you by banging on the crib railing and crowing loudly. Later you may see her standing at the coffee table, pounding on the top, and uttering a string of babbles. She is feeling very proud of her upright status.

Parents frequently ask whether playpens are a good idea for the ten month old baby. The answer is "Maybe." On the one hand, the ten month old baby is learning about space and objects, and being confined in a playpen would hamper her explorations. On the other hand, for babies who have just learned to pull up, the playpen is a safe place to practice. Also, there are times when parents can't keep their eyes on the baby and safety becomes the number one issue. For the most part, playpens are not very useful unless they are used creatively. You may want to use the playpen with one side down as a place for the baby to practice climbing, to store her toys, or to practice her throwing skills.

When reaching and grasping, ten month olds can carry on tasks involving coordination of shoulder, arm, wrist and fingers, such as taking the cover off a box or standing up a toy dog. If an object is placed in front of your baby, she reaches for it directly and picks it up deftly with forefinger and thumb. This smooth grasp movement seems to be accompanied by a slight turning or tilting of the wrist that takes place in the first phase of the reach. At a younger age your baby learned to use the pincer movement for picking up crumbs from her high chair. She had also learned to rotate her wrist, inspecting a toy in her hand. Now we see your baby gaining new control and efficiency by putting these skills together.

Your baby's new level of efficiency may be demonstrated in a new skill—tearing. She can grasp the thin pages of a magazine or phone book and then rip them by rotating her wrist. Similarly, your baby may now be interested in stacking one small block on another. In order to accomplish this feat, baby must lift a block up with her thumb and forefinger, place it on top of a second block, and then let go at just the right moment. If baby succeeds, chances are that she will not rest on her laurels. Instead, she will place a third block on top of the second with the outcome, of course, the inevitable crash of the tower.

Seeing, Hearing, and Feeling

An adult recognizes that, despite appearances, things do not get smaller as they move further away. We could hold a coffee cup in our hand and identify a same-sized coffee cup on the other side of the room. This ability to compensate for distance when we estimate size is called size constancy. Although some psychologists believe that infants have a built-in capacity to estimate size, it takes practice with space and objects before this capacity is fully developed. The behavior of a ten month old may provide clues that indicate she is acquiring a notion of size constancy. A large dog that she sees for the first time will frighten her even when it is across the room, but she may be quite willing to play with a little dog that comes up to her.

The ten month old's awareness of how things are supposed to look is demonstrated in many different ways. If you hand her a drinking cup upside down, she immediately turns it over. When her sister does a head stand, she watches her and laughs. She can also recognize a familiar object when she sees just a small part of it. She picks up a spoon almost covered by a napkin and puts it directly into her mouth.

With sounds as with sights, the baby's perceptions continue to sharpen. She's getting quite good at telling which direction a sound is coming from. If a sound is made behind her back, she turns around immediately and looks at the place it came from. She can easily recognize members of the family by voice alone, and can identify subtle differences in voice tone that show anger, teasing, calmness, joy, or annoyance.

At nine months old the baby was especially interested in emptying out containers. At ten months, she is just as interested in how containers get filled up. She sticks her fingers into her own nose and mouth, places rings on top of a spindle, and fits miniature characters into toy furniture. The problem that baby is most likely to be preoccupied with is what fits into what. She will use both hands and make grunting noises, for example, as she attempts to put a large measuring cup inside a smaller one. When her efforts to fit things together fail, the baby may hand both objects to an adult in a wordless request for assistance.

Your baby shows a new ability to solve problems involving the relationship of "behind" or "inside." If you hold a toy behind a lucite tray, she is likely to reach around the barrier to get the toy. A short time ago she would have tried to reach through the tray to retrieve the object. You will see the same progression with a toy that is placed inside a clear container with a lid on it. Earlier your baby tried to get the toy by reaching either through the side or through the lid. Now she will push the lid off and reach inside to get her toy.

Another "container skill" that your baby may be interested in is dropping. At a younger age, when your baby dropped a toy, it was quite by accident. A few months later your baby mastered the act of purposeful dropping. She was able to let go of one toy in order to take hold of another. Perhaps she enjoyed playing a game of dropping food and toys off her highchair. Now at ten months old your baby is able to conduct deliberate experiments with dropping. She can hold her hand above a container, intentionally release a bunch of keys, and listen to the clatter as they hit the bottom of the pan.

Knowing Your Baby

The ten month old baby is usually friendly and outgoing. She uses her vocabulary of babbles to carry on a new conversation and enjoys experimenting with all kinds of new sound effects. She is becoming a good mimic and will try to copy sounds and words that are not in her repertoire yet. She has probably learned to understand several words, and will show off her routines in front of a familiar audience. These routines may consist of word action games like, "Show Mommy your eyes," "Throw Daddy a kiss," or "Play pat-a-cake with Nana."

The intense attachment to parents that characterizes the infant from six to nine months may show some signs of change. As creeping becomes easy and automatic, and as the baby finds that she can get back to her starting point, she gets braver about letting Mother out of her sight. She now sees herself as a free agent, venturing across or out of the room and exploring new terrain. During her longer expeditions, baby may take along a favorite blanket or toy. This toy or blanket becomes a security object that helps baby break old ties and gain independence.

When parent and baby are not on home territory there is a definite change in exploratory behavior. At first the baby will restrict her play area to within touching distance of her parent. Even when she has worked up the courage to cross the room, the baby will check back with eyes and voice to make sure that Mommy stays put. Mom or Dad provide the baby with a base of security that permits exploration within limits.

Some babies do not feel brave about exploring even when their parent is on the scene. If a new person enters the room they are likely to attach themselves to a parent's leg and retain their "leg hold" until the visitor departs. When a parent is successful in getting away for a brief period, the baby will react to their return with a combination of clinging and angry behavior.

For babies who are reluctant to venture out, it is helpful to practice leave-taking behavior. You can begin with a game of peek-a-boo in which you hide under a blanket. When your baby has learned to enjoy the peek-a-boo game, the next step is hiding in the room. At first you can reappear instantly with a happy, "Hi, Baby." After a while, wait a few seconds and then reappear. Once your baby is accustomed to disappearance acts in the room, try extending the game to outside of the room. A relative, a sibling, or a close friend can also be helpful in encouraging the baby's explorations. When the baby is left behind with someone she knows, it is much easier to say goodbye to a parent.

Having a substitute caregiver whom the baby loves and trusts is especially important if parents have to leave the baby for an extended period. Many studies have been done on babies in day care with essentially the same outcome. If a baby is given loving care by a consistent caregiver, and if a baby continues to receive quality care at home, she will make a good adjustment to a day care situation.

An alternative to a child care facility is a babysitter. Usually the best situation is to have the babysitter in your home. Before leaving your baby with a strange sitter, have the sitter come to your house once or twice while you are home so that she becomes familiar.

If you are in a situation in which the most logical solution is child care in the sitter's home, easing the baby into the situation is particularly important. It often helps to bring along familiar things such as a huggee, a blanket, or a favorite toy. It also helps for you to stay at the sitter's home for at least one sitting. As your baby sees you interacting happily with the sitter, she will gain confidence in her own ability to cope.

A ten month old baby is able to predict what is going to happen in a home setting. In a new setting she has no way of predicting what might happen next, and it's natural for her to feel less secure. If your baby has not been left much with a substitute caregiver, you can anticipate that she will be fearful of a new child care center or babysitter. Once you are assured that a substitute caregiver is competent and is interested in playing with your baby, be consistent and cheerful in the way you say goodbye. In time your baby will establish a new set of predictions, and separation fears will resolve themselves.

Even when your baby has become quite independent during the day, you will see signs of clinginess at night. Baby recognizes that being separated at night from her parents is not the same as being separated during the day. At night, she is stuck in the crib and there is no way to simply change directions and rediscover her parents. Parents solve this sleep time problem in different ways depending on their personal style. Some parents hold the baby until she falls asleep and then put her down in the crib. Other parents prefer to rely on bedtime routines, giving the baby a huggee, singing, patting and giving last kisses until the baby allows them to leave. Still other parents do not want to get the baby in a habit they will not be able to break later. They put their baby in the crib cheerfully but firmly, and endure the cries of distress as their baby settles down. There is no one right way for parents to solve this recurring sleep problem. Each family must search out an alternative that works well with their baby.

Setting the Stage

The ten month old is ready for variety. No matter how many interesting things there are to do inside, the baby really needs to have some outside time. A ride in the car, an excursion to the grocery store, a visit with a relative or playmate are important for mothers and babies alike.

By now the baby may be ready for some "structured" playtime where Mom and Dad put aside some time just to play with baby. Daddy's time is especially important, because Dads and Moms tend to have different play styles. Fathers are more likely to rough house and help their baby exercise. Mothers are more likely to focus on intellectual experiences. Both kinds of play are important.

Playtime

Making Discoveries:

Tube Talk

Disguise your voice by talking through a cardboard tube. You will be surprised at baby's attention. Now be silly—make some sounds . . . ba-ba-ba or ma-ma-ma! Give a tube to the baby. Maybe she will imitate those sounds.

Baby Blocks

Make a series of red cardboard blocks and one yellow one. (Contact paper on pint size milk cartons works well.) Place a bell inside the yellow block. See if your baby can learn to discriminate color by picking out the block with the bell.

Poke Box

Babies love to poke their fingers into tiny places. Here is an activity that utilizes this skill. Punch out two finger holes in the sides of a small, thin box. Line the box with different textures—fur, burlap, velvet, or sandpaper. Show the baby how to poke her finger in a hole. (You can poke your finger in the other hole.) Discuss how it feels—soft, rough, bumpy. This is a great game to take in the car!

Seek and Find

Hide a clock or radio under a pillow. Baby's listening skills will strengthen as she attempts to discover the clock.

Let Baby Keep Time to Music

Make the baby a cereal box drum. Give her a wooden spoon to use as a drum stick. Encourage her to use it for banging.

Car Ride

Show your baby how to push a small car or truck along the floor. After a while your baby will learn to let go so that the car rolls by itself.

Table Banging

Bring in another baby, and let them share in a table banging game.

Play a Telephone Game

Talk to the baby on her play telephone—give her a turn. As the baby plays the telephone game, she learns the fun of carrying on a conversation. Unplugging a real phone works even better, but has some drawbacks. Your baby may want to return to her game when the phone has not been pulled out.

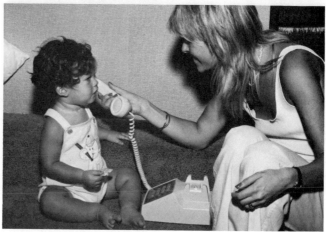

Magazine Tearing

Some babies at ten months are ready for tearing. Old magazines, tissue paper, wrapping paper or foil provide interesting tearing experiences. Remember that your baby may also want to discover what the paper tastes like. Tearing activities require close supervision. If your baby is more interested in stuffing a wad of paper in her mouth than tearing it, reserve this activity for a later month.

Improving Coordination:

Sticks and Stones

Your outdoor environment provides you with an array of objects for baby to manipulate. Encourage her to gather stones in a pail—twigs or even leaves. Not only will it aid her fine motor coordination, it will also stimulate her sense of touch.

Paper Pull

Cut some contact paper into strips. Pull the backing off and stick it partly to a table. Start pulling the strip off—Baby will soon catch on. It's almost as much fun as peeling labels off of jars and bottles!

Follow the Leader

This is an age when your baby loves to imitate. Play follow the leader with your baby, using simple gestures or hand play. Tap the table, open and close your fist, or put a hat on your head! Always talk about the things you are doing.

Tube Balance

Place a small inflated tube in front of your baby. Give her some small blocks. Demonstrate how to line the blocks on the tube. The wobbly surface strengthens her awareness of balance and improves her coordination. A tube is also great for the bath—dropping things into the center can be an endless game.

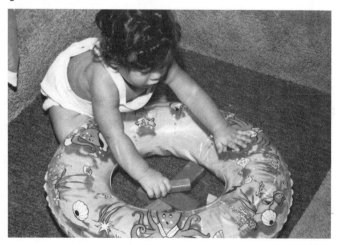

Spindle Toy

Make a spindle toy by inserting a cardboard tube from a toilet paper roll into the plastic top of a coffee can. Show your baby how to place a plastic bracelet over the spindle.

Reaching for Fun

If your baby is pulling up to a standing position, place favorite toys on a low table so that baby will have to stretch to reach them. This will give her practice in reaching and will add to her spatial awareness.

Triple Feat

Give your baby a third toy when she has a toy in each hand. See if she can figure out how to hold all three toys.

Solving Problems:

Nesting

Your baby learns about size as she experiments with different objects. Measuring cups are excellent for demonstrating a sequence of size. Begin with two—then add more!

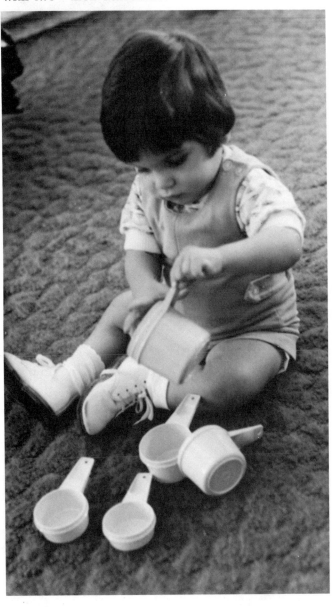

Two and One

Cover three boxes, two square ones and one round one, with the same contact paper. Place cracker crumbs inside the round box. Will baby discover that the round box holds the crackers?

Clothespin Drop

A handful of clothespins and a plastic bottle will help baby learn how to fill and empty a container. She will need help at first, especially when it is time to empty the container. Later, vary the containers . . . an empty oatmeal container or coffee can will add to the fun!

Hiding Pictures

When Daddy is away it is fun to hide his picture. Where can he be? Under baby's dinner plate? Maybe in the toy box? In baby's shoe or even in his favorite book? Whenever it is discovered, shout "Daddy " Soon your baby will join in the fun! Other pictures can be substituted but don't change too quickly, or you will confuse your baby.

Find the Toy

Put a small toy inside a paper bag or box. As your baby struggles to get it out she will increase her understanding of inside and outside.

Curlers

Give your baby hair rollers of two different sizes. See if she is interested in placing one inside of the other.

Toy Tie

Tie a string on to the toys that your baby plays with in the high chair with one end of the string tied to the high chair arm or tray. Trying to pull the toy back with the string will be a real challenge.

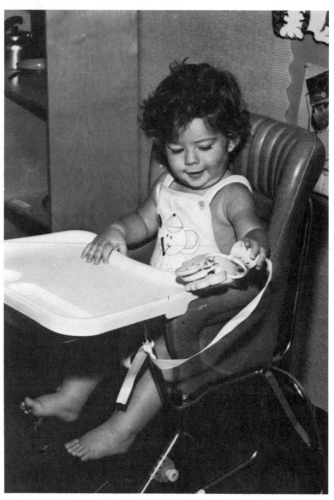

Where is Sister?

Show your baby two family photos (e.g. brother and sister). Cover both photos with a cloth. Ask the baby to find brother and then sister. You will be surprised at how much your baby understands.

Daily Routines

Mealtime:

It All Stacks Up

All those empty kitchen containers—cereal boxes, juice cans, butter bowls, or egg cartons—will make wonderful castles and bridges for your inquisitive ten month old. They will teach her the laws of balance and weight as they wobble and tumble before her eyes!

Storehouse

Those kitchen building blocks need a place to live. Reserve a cabinet for baby to house her mealtime games in. Putting them away can be half the fun.

Buy Your Baby a Sassy Seat

A sassy seat makes mealtime more pleasant for a ten month old, especially if you go out to a restaurant. With a sassy seat your baby can sit up at the table and will stay contented for a longer time. There are some disadvantages, of course. You can't feel safe with a table cloth. Nor can you be sure that the food won't be tossed on the floor. (A plastic cloth spread out on the floor solves the clean-up problem.)

Restaurant "Survival Kit"

If you do take your baby to a restaurant it's a good idea to take along a snack. Cracker bits, cheese bits, or unsweetened cold cereal in a paper bag works well. Even if the snack doesn't interest your baby, she will enjoy the challenge of reaching into the bag.

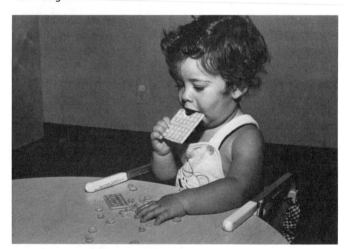

Bathtime:

Bubble Blower

Bubbles are fun, and your baby will enjoy blowing bubbles with a straw in her *clean* bath water. You blow through a straw and your baby will imitate.

Directions

Your baby is not too young to follow simple directions. She will be proud to—Wash her tummy—Wash her toes!

Rain Rain

The bathtub is a good place to make rain. A small empty plastic container can easily be turned into a rain maker . . . just punch some holes in it with an ice pick. Let baby fill it then hold it up—Look out for the storm!

**Washcloth
Gifts**

Wrapping a tub toy up in a washcloth adds a little mystery to the baby's bath. Encourage her to unwrap the wet cloth and discover her toy. Soon she'll be wrapping up some gifts for you.

Quiet Time:

Sand Man

Darken the room and turn on a flashlight. Move the light slowly around the room. Your baby will attempt to follow the light as it moves. Then, after a while, she may drop off to sleep.

Goodnight
Record

Put a record on before your baby falls asleep. Turn down the volume as your baby closes her eyes.

ELEVEN MONTHS

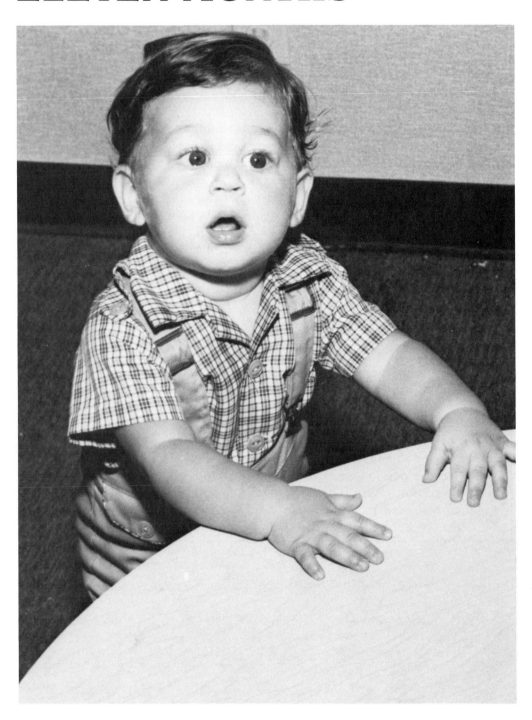

Baby's Viewpoint: In the last chapter we talked about how the ten month old baby had learned the actions that go with certain stereotyped phrases: "throw a kiss," "pat-a-cake," "how big is the baby?" Now we see the baby's understanding of language going beyond this vocabulary of action phrases. The baby is able to break apart a phrase and attend to simple words. Although he is unlikely to say more than one or two words, the baby has become much more proficient at understanding the meaning of these words.

Now that your baby is interested in attaching meaning to single words, reading books is likely to be a favorite activity. Most babies show preferences for certain books. Cloth books, despite their advantages in terms of durability, are likely to be discarded. The pictures are just too dull. Books with glossy sturdy pages and very bright pictures, or books with interesting textures are likely to be selected as favorites.

At first when your baby reads a book he will play with it much as he plays with a toy, pulling at the pages, turning it in all directions and bouncing it on the floor. Only when these experiments are over will your baby be ready to focus on the contents.

Activity books, like "Pat The Bunny" or "Touch Me," provide a good transition between a toy and a book. Baby can look at the pictures, listen to the words and at the same time pat a piece of cotton, poke his finger in a hole, or find a bunny hidden under a piece of fabric.

When your baby seems ready to enjoy a picture book, make sure to select a book with objects that are familiar to your baby. Some babies enjoy looking at books with large pictures: a telephone, a ball, a teddy bear, or a set of keys. Other babies like to find a picture of a particular character, such as E.T., Smurfette or Mickey Mouse, who appears in different places on each page of the book. Although parents quite naturally like to read a book to a baby while he is sitting on their lap, babies may resist a position where they can't watch the parent's face. Try sitting on the floor with your baby facing you and the book facing toward the baby. This way the baby can watch your face and the book at the same time.

Motor Skills

While some babies at eleven months are still getting around on their hands and knees, and others are walking by themselves, most babies by this time can walk by holding on to a parent's hand or by pulling themselves up on furniture and cruising from spot to spot. When the baby first begins to walk, he holds both hands out like wings to help him balance and spreads his legs, bends his knees, and leans slightly forward. After some practice, he learns to use only one hand for balance and to hold a toy in the other. As soon as possible the baby will cram toys into both hands. In fact, he seems to be trying to find out how many toys he can carry at one time.

Seeing, Hearing, and Feeling

The eleven month old baby enjoys new sights and sounds. A trip to the supermarket, for example, is an exciting experience. Baby will enjoy discovering the sound of a macaroni box when it is shaken, the feel of a banana, or the smell of a melon. Some babies are adventurous with new tastes—they may surprise you at their willingness to sample a mushroom or bite into a piece of cauliflower. If the baby becomes too restless you can bring a nourishing snack from home—cheese, grapes, or a favorite cracker.

Most eleven month old babies enjoy feeling different textures with their feet as well as their hands. Your baby will still show many of the same preferences he had as an infant. Some babies suddenly develop a strong dislike for certain textures. For instance, they may not like the feel of sand on their feet and will refuse to walk barefoot on a beach or in a sandbox, or they may react negatively to putting their hands in something wet and sticky, like finger paint, jello or yogurt. These strong dislikes signal an increased sensitivity to tactile experiences. If your baby is especially sensitive to different feels, introduce new experiences gradually in a modified form. Put a little powder on the floor and let him touch it with his feet, or put a dab of yogurt on his index finger. As the baby experiences these more mild sensations, he will be less easily disturbed by differences in textures.

Because your baby learns so much about his world through a sense of feel, a variety of experiences are important. Allow your baby to walk barefoot whenever possible. He will enjoy discovering the coldness of bathroom tile, the roughness of carpeting, or the smoothness of wood. Contrary to popular belief, the baby does not need shoes for support when he first begins to walk.

By eleven months of age your baby has a good understanding of spatial relationships like "inside" and "behind." He knows when he is taking part in a "hide the toy" game, and he is much harder to fool. At a younger age when you moved a toy from one hiding place to another, he searched for it in the place where you hid it the first time. Now, he watches your hand carefully and goes right to the second hiding place.

Placing one object inside another can still be a difficult task, however. Given two tin cans that differ in size, the baby decides which tin can fits into the other on a trial and error basis. The larger can may be banged against the smaller with a real show of strength before baby is convinced that it will not fit inside.

Simply placing small objects in a larger container presents an easier challenge and may turn into a virtual obsession. Over and over again, baby will drop these items into the container, take them out and then drop them in again. A parent watching the activity will lose interest long before the infant, who repeats the task with obvious purpose and enjoyment.

Knowing Your Baby

The baby's ability to communicate leaps forward between ten and twelve months old. At a younger age the baby's major communications were associated with feelings. In a variety of ways your baby told you when he was feeling happy or sad, silly or whiny, restless or contented. During the last quarter of the first year the baby is able to communicate some very specific messages. Parents who are with their baby all the time may not be as aware as "outsiders" of these changes in baby's communication skills. Often we get the best descriptions of new language events from a visiting friend or grandparent. Here are some typical reports from proud and observant grandmothers.

Rosemary is so smart, you won't believe it. I took her in the swimming pool and she loved it. When I brought her inside to dress her, I had her standing by the window. She looked outside and saw the pool, and got all excited. She pulled at the neck of her romper suit, pointed to the pool, and made these real urgent "oh oh" sounds. She was really trying to let me know that she wanted to go back in the pool.

I know you won't believe me, but Nicholas is really beginning to talk. He says "ba ba" when he wants to play ball, "da da" when he sees a dog, and "mmm" when he sees his mother making supper. And when I read him the Three Bears story, and we come to the page where Goldilocks eats the porridge, everytime we come to it, Nicholas says "mmm."

Your baby is also becoming more interested in the names of objects. On a trip to the grocery store, you can point out certain items on the shelves, such as milk, bananas, bread, or cereal. On a car ride or when watching television, your baby will enjoy looking for a few favorite objects: dogs, trucks, cows, etc. Eleven month old babies recognize key words in more and more phrases, including song phrases like "pop goes the weasel" or "all fall down." When you sing the song, your baby will perform the appropriate action.

Despite the fact that your baby does not always perform on cue, you will continue to see signs of growing sociability. By now your baby will have made friends with quite a few different adults. Though they cannot compete with Mom and Dad, familiar adults are honored with a special greeting. A common way for your baby to acknowledge familiar adults is to offer them a toy.

Now that your baby is expanding his repertoire of social skills, he is quite insistent about being where the action is. If family and friends are sitting at the table, he wants to be there, too. If his car seat is in the back seat and a passenger is riding in the front seat, he objects vociferously. These demands are not always easy to comply with. A sassy seat is a good way to bring baby up to the table if your table has the right kind of edge. The car problem can be solved by playing a singing game or providing your baby with a "steering wheel" so he can take part in the driving.

Although increased social skills for most babies make it easier to leave them with a sitter, some eleven month old babies are even "clingier" than they were at eight months. They appear to be on constant vigil, making sure that their parents don't slip out of their sight. Eventually this behavior passes as children have time to overcome fears of separation.

In the last chapter we talked about sleep problems that appear toward the end of the first year. Sleep problems may be cyclical. Just as parents feel secure about getting a full night's sleep, something else happens and their sleep is interrupted.

If your baby will not sleep through the night, and a diaper change or a drink does nothing to calm him down, you may want to solve the problem by putting the baby into your own bed. On the other hand, you may not want to start such a habit. An alternative is to stay in the baby's room and rock, pat or sing him back to sleep.

Setting the Stage

Driving in the Car

Your baby enjoys a car ride but will not fall asleep in the car as quickly as he did at a younger age. String large beads or hair rollers across his car seat to help him enjoy the ride.

Taking the Baby Grocery Shopping

Grocery shopping usually works out well for an eleven month old baby. You can talk to your baby about what he is seeing and give him a turn tossing small items in the basket. Remember, if you give him a snack in the grocery store you may be beginning a habit that is difficult to break.

Making New Adult Friends

Although your baby may still not want you out of sight, he enjoys making new adult friends as long as he can make the overtures. Your baby will warm up faster to new people if they start off by offering him a toy.

Going to a Restaurant

Parents as well as babies enjoy an occasional meal out. Unfortunately, your baby at eleven months may be in the throwing food stage and taking him to a restaurant may present problems. Possible solutions include bringing along a sassy seat so that your baby can sit right up at the table, bringing along a bag of toys or nutritious snack foods that will capture your baby's interest, or choosing a fast food restaurant that is set up for "food throwing" babies.

Playing With Other Children

Your baby is ready to spend time with other children. If he has older siblings or neighbors he will watch what they are playing with and attempt to get hold of it. With babies his own age he will start by playing along side them. After a while he will get to know them. When babies know each other you will see them watching each other's faces and even sharing a toy.

Playtime

Feed the Puppet

Put your hand inside an animal hand puppet. Give the baby a ball. Ask the baby to feed the puppet. After a couple of demonstrations your baby will understand your words.

Little Daddy

Give your baby a comb and a baby doll. See if he will comb the doll's hair.

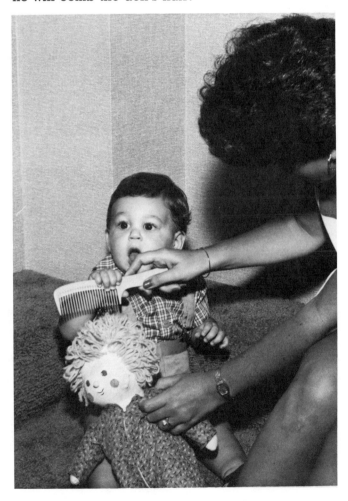

Humor

The eleven month old baby is developing a sense of humor and will laugh at an incongruous event. Pretend to drink from his bottle or put on his shoe. Did your baby burst out laughing?

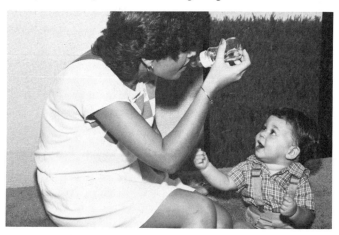

Out the Window

When you hear an airplane or a bird, take the baby to the window and talk about what you see.

Making Discoveries:

Beat Rhythms With a Spoon

Let the baby beat out rhythms with a wooden spoon on the back of a pan or a pie plate.

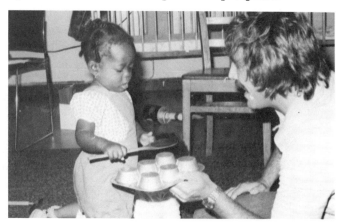

**Roll Toy
Through
Tunnel**

Roll a toy car through a cardboard tube. See if the baby will watch for it to come out the other end.

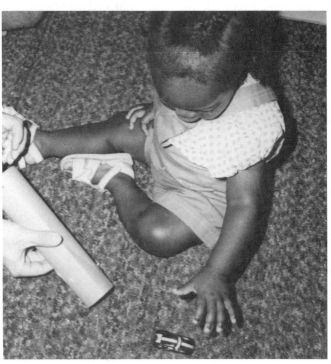

**Put Hand
Puppet on Baby**

Give the baby a hand puppet and let him manipulate it.

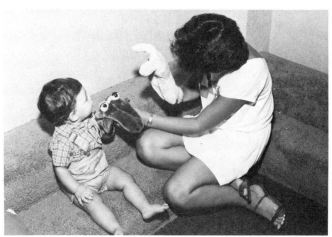

Tie Ribbons on Baby's Toys

Tie different color ribbons to two of the baby's favorite toys, e.g., car and teddy. Put the toys in front of him so that he has to pull the ribbons to get them. Ask him to give you the teddy—then the car. When he learns to pull the right strings with the toy in view, try the game with first one toy hidden and then both toys hidden.

Lever Play

Your baby is learning how to push down a lever. Let him practice with a top or a riding car with a "shift."

Improving Coordination:

Balance Beam

Place a well sanded board (or ironing board) on the floor. It should be at least six inches wide and four feet long. Place a toy at one end and baby at the other end. By crawling or walking with help he will retrieve the toy. An inclined board also lends itself to this activity.

Sticky Stuff

Pull the back off a large piece of contact paper. Tape it on the floor with the sticky side up. Let the baby walk across it. Place some light toys on it—baby will enjoy pulling them off. Those arm and leg muscles will be used more than you think. Take the baby away before he gets frustrated.

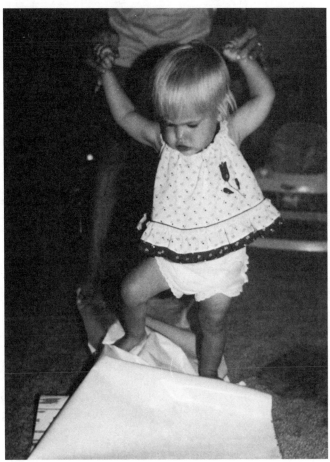

Help Baby Slide Downstairs

If the baby has learned how to climb upstairs, show him how to slide downstairs on his stomach, feet first. (It is better to show the baby a safe way to come down stairs than to count on keeping a gate closed.)

Use Chair as a Walker

If the baby is walking, show him how to hold on to a light-weight chair and push it around the room.

Let Baby Push His Stroller

If the baby is an early walker, let him push his own stroller. It's a great balance exercise and gives baby practice with starting and stopping. (A light stroller will be more stable if you weigh it down with a heavy book.)

Underfoot

Whether your baby is walking on his own or holding on to your hand, he will enjoy the experience of walking on different surfaces. Give him a chance to walk barefoot on carpet, floor, sand and grass.

Solving Problems:

Put Crackers in a Film Can

Place bits of crackers or cereal inside a small, screw-top film container or plastic jar. Place the lid top on loosely (do not turn). Show the baby how to take off the lid and retrieve the crumbs.

Play Ball-Rolling Games

Roll a ball to the baby and encourage him to roll it back. This activity can be done rhythmically with a chant:

We roll the ball, it's rolling,
Now roll it down the track.
We roll it down to Baby,
And Baby rolls it back.

Wrap Up Toys

Wrap up toys in foil or tissue paper and allow the baby to unwrap. Do not use tape or ribbon.

Cold Stuff

After grocery shopping, leave a few things out of the refrigerator for your baby to put away. Talk about how cold an item is and let baby feel what cold is. Let your baby help put cold items in the refrigerator.

Make Baby a Tote Bag

Make your baby a flannel tote bag to wear over his shoulder. Let him reach inside and get different toys.

Shoes On

Give your baby a pair of your shoes and let him practice putting them on.

Pet Play

If you are planning to get a pet for your baby, this is a good age to do it. Your baby is not strong enough to hurt the pet and will enjoy playing with it. By the time your baby is old enough to accidentally hurt the pet, the pet will be used to the baby and will be able to protect itself.

Stand-Up Toys   Give the baby a stuffed animal that sits up. Place the animal on its side and see if the baby will place it back in a sitting position.

Daily Routines

Mealtime:

Pouring   Paper cups and Cheerios make good pouring tools. They are not as messy as water but achieve the same results. Fill a cup with Cheerios. Show the baby how to pour it into another cup—then another cup. Baby will enjoy sampling those that spill.

Flour Paint   Writing is magic when we use flour instead of pencil. Spread a thin layer of flour on a clean smooth surface. Demonstrate how to rub your finger in the flour and make circles, zig zags and slashes.

Crackers

Let your baby spread jelly on his own crackers, or decorate a peanut butter cracker with Cheerios. Doing jobs for himself gives him a feeling of power.

Serving Bowl

If you're serving mashed potatoes, corn or other vegetables, let your baby try and take a scoop out and place it on his plate—you'll be surprised what he may try to sample if he is allowed to help.

Cup and Spoon

A single cup and tablespoon will challenge the baby's filling ability. Show him how to dip the spoon in a bowl of water and fill the cup. It's an endless game with no mess involved. Small bits of ice will add to the interest and the challenge.

Bathtime:

Duck Soup

Water play is always a valuable experience for your baby. Utilizing different containers will teach the baby about space and volume. Introduce him to a soup strainer and ladle. Place some small floating ducks in the tub. You and your baby can lean over the tub and try and catch some of the ducks. It is a good way to practice eye-hand coordination.

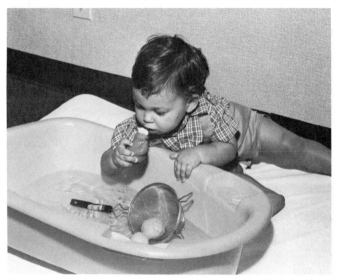

Wall Washing

Give your baby a sponge and let him clean the tub. He will enjoy making circles and up and down strokes.

Scoop and Catch!

Give your baby a flour scoop and some small bath toys. Catching the toys with the flour scoop will improve his eye-hand coordination.

Self-Help

Give your baby a toothbrush and see if he will try to brush his own teeth.

Diapertime:

Sticker Fun

The difficult time of diapering becomes a little easier if you let your baby decorate a diaper with stickers. He'll enjoy putting them on the new diaper and you'll be glad to get that clean diaper in place.

Baby Diapers

Make a small cloth diaper for a small teddy bear. Sew velcro tabs on each side. Give your baby a turn putting the diaper on his teddy bear. It will make diaper time more fun.

Tape and Tape

When your baby is especially wiggly on the changing table, sometimes a piece of scotch tape is a good distractor. The fun of putting it on and taking it off will last at least as long as it takes to diaper your baby.

Quiet Time:

Squeaking Pictures

Make your baby a squeaking picture book. As you turn the pages, let your baby make the pictures squeak. (Squeaks can be bought at novelty stores and glued or sewed under pieces of fabric in your home-made picture books.)

Zipper Baby

Dress a doll or bear in an outfit with a zipper. Show baby how the zipper goes up and down, or opens and closes. Baby is beginning to develop some simple self-help skills.

Mitt Play

Large cumbersome gloves make an excellent problem solving activity. By trial and error baby will discover how to put his hand in the glove. He may carry out an experiment and put the glove on his foot.

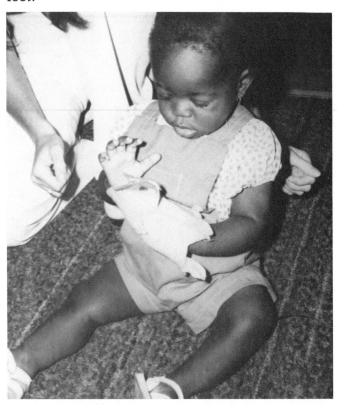

Car Songs

Songs that are familiar are especially useful on a car ride. Your baby may resist staying in his carseat and you will find that he can be quieted with a simple jingle.

TWELVE MONTHS

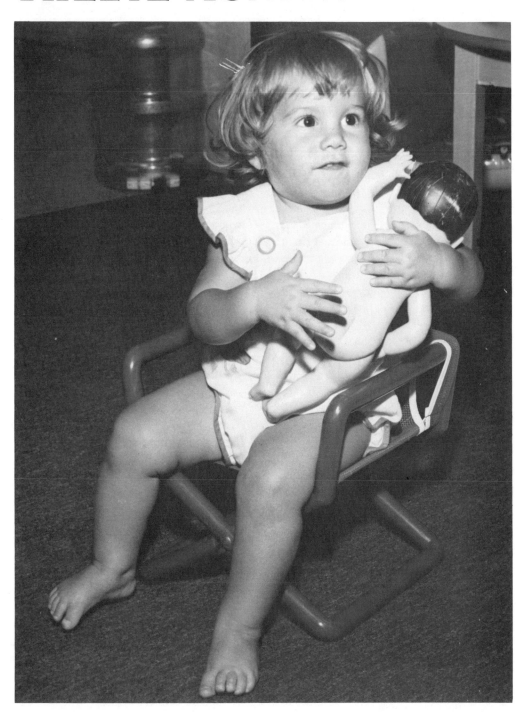

Baby's Viewpoint: A favorite photo in many a family album is the picture of baby on her first birthday with both hands plunged into the cake. The need for active exploration that prompted that dive into the icing explains much of baby's behavior. From the moment of birth your baby has been actively taking in information about her environment. In the beginning months her explorations were limited to searching with her eyes, listening to sounds and identifying new sensations. From three to six months her explorations were extended as she reached out with her hands, manipulated objects and playfully fingered her parent's face. During the second half of the first year your baby learned to crawl, creep, and pull to a standing position and her field of exploration expanded.

As your baby launches into her second year of life, you will notice a subtle difference in the way she explores her environment. Her active explorations are turning into experiments. She is not only interested in dumping out the contents of Mother's purse, she is looking for new ways to accomplish it. She may start off on the floor beside the purse, pulling out objects one at a time. Pretty soon she sticks both hands into the purse and scoops out the contents. As a final maneuver, she stands up, purse in hand, turns it over and watches the contents spill out over the floor.

The same kind of experimentation that we see going on with objects is even more striking with people. Your baby is becoming aware of her ability to create a reaction and, during a social exchange, she is likely to play to her audience. A few months ago she would hand an object to a visitor and take it back again in a kind of social game. Now, we can see an element of teasing creeping into her back and forth games. Baby will spontaneously offer a cookie to a visitor. As soon as the visitor goes to bite the cookie, the baby whisks away her hand and smiles impishly. Her intent to tease is unmistakeable.

This increased awareness of people's behavior is also evident in your baby's imitative skills. Now your baby imitates not only the actions you model, but actions that you are unaware of. She may wipe her high chair tray after a spill, or mimic adults who absentmindedly are tapping their fingers, or pulling on an ear lobe. She will especially enjoy making faces and will copy a scowl or a crinkled up nose.

A careful observation of the year old baby reveals signs of imaginative play. This pretending, which is still highly imitative, gives us a glimpse of what is to come. Mother feels sorry for baby's doll when it falls on the floor. She picks the doll up and gives it some love. A little later baby is seen hugging and kissing the doll. Mother pushes a toy car around the edge of the bathtub, making race car noises, and the next night baby does the same thing. Your baby's ability to re-enact a familiar scene or experience represents an important advance in the development of thought. You will have many opportunities to encourage this development in the months ahead.

Motor Skills

At a year old, most babies have become quite adept at getting around the house, even if they haven't learned to walk. Babies seem interested not only in what is in front of them or behind them, but also in things that are out of reach. Many babies climb on anything they can pull themselves on top of, although they are never as good at getting down from things as they are getting up. As they become more adept at climbing up on things, they may become increasingly fearful about getting down. This is not a regression. It is just that with this awareness comes a new respect for high places and a new awareness of danger.

Bath time may be used now to practice some motor skills. Baby is not only splashing with her hands, but her feet too may get into the act. Your baby may also try standing up in the bath; or even climbing out. No-skid strips on the bottom of the tub makes bath time a little safer.

Although the twelve month old may have just mastered the art of walking, she may already be combining her walking with other skills. She may walk and pull, walk and push, or walk and carry toys at the same time. If there is an older sibling around to imitate she may even try some gymnastics. She will put her head on the floor in a mock sommersault, and then look around for applause. Another motor skill your baby is practicing is throwing. Sometimes she throws for the sheer joy of it. At other times she is especially interested in where the ball is going. She throws the ball gently to Daddy two or three times and then tries a bigger throw in a different direction. With rapt attention, she watches the ball bounce off the wall or down the steps. She follows the ball as it rolls through the bedroom door or under the bed.

If the climate permits, swimming is a delightful activity for a twelve month old. Most babies feel quite comfortable about putting their head in the water, and a back and forth swim between Mom and Dad is one of their favorite activities. Babies also enjoy a swim tube seat where they can glide across the pool and splash with their hands. Swim rings should not be used for the one year old because it is much too easy to slip through the hole.

Enrolling a twelve month old in a swimming class may increase the baby's skills, although it is very unlikely that the baby will become a true swimmer. Because the baby still tends to be wary of strangers, it is preferable for parents to be with their babies during swim lessons. The principle benefits of any early swimming program is that it can help babies feel more relaxed in the water. If your baby is frightened by formal lessons, even when you are present, they ought to be stopped.

Seeing, Hearing, and Feeling

The baby loves to experiment with new sensations, wet slimy jello, sticky icing, or hard cold ice cubes. Keeping her hands out of her food during mealtime is just about impossible. She splashes the oatmeal, smears the apple juice and dips her fingers into the orange juice. Even the most finicky parents abandon their struggle to keep the baby clean.

Differences in sounds are just as interesting to your baby as differences in texture. She will tap a spoon against a glass, a plate, a bowl, or her high chair. She tries different vocalizations such as a shout, a string of jabbers that sounds like talking, or a kind of sing-song. She may awaken in the morning and practice her jabbers for a good twenty minutes before calling out for attention.

Your baby's "scientific" experiments and investigations are probably most apparent when she is playing with objects. Favorite activities now include stirring with a spoon, inverting a container to pour out the contents, or pulling a toy by a string. All these investigations have in common the fact that your baby, on a primitive level, is learning to use a tool.

Baby's ability to experiment is fortified by a new level of strength and a new determination to find out if things come apart. Instead of playing with the suction toy on her high chair, she will pull and push at it until she can finally yank if off. Baby tries harder than ever to make objects go back together again, to get the blocks back into the shape sorter, to reconnect a set of pop beads.

Although your twelve month old may sometimes feel frustrated when objects won't do her bidding, her repertoire of accomplishments is growing. She may be able to transfer a spoonful of food, hold on to a cup, or open a small box of raisins. Probably she is learning how to scoop up water with a bath toy, pull a shoe lace until it unties, pick a leaf off a plant, slip a necklace over her head, scribble with a pencil, and open up a cabinet by pulling on the knob.

Knowing Your Baby

By a year old, most babies have mastered their first word, and will use it on every possible occasion. This word is really more than just a word. It represents a whole sentence. "Mommy" means, "Mommy, come in and get me." "Ba-ba" may mean, "I want my bottle—right now!" Although babies at this age cannot say more than three or four words, the twelve month old understands language quite well. Your baby knows the names of everyone in the family and will look toward the person whose name is called. She may even point out pictures of the family members in a photograph album. And when you use a phrase like "Do you want a cookie?", your baby's response is quite different from her response to "Time for your medicine." Some parents actually resort to spelling, instead of saying "bedtime" or "going out."

As your baby's ability to understand language grows, she will learn to follow simple directions. Typically babies will learn the meaning of one or two common phrases, like "Give me," "Show me," or "Hand me." Once your baby has learned these key phrases, she will learn to follow several different commands like "Show me your eyes," "Show me your belly button," "Show me your toys," "Get Mommy's purse," or "Get Mommy's keys."

Although babies are delighted with their ability to follow directions, the one year old baby may also learn how to tease. When you ask her to hand you something, she may start to go for it, but then bring you something else. The fact that she is watching your reaction and smiling broadly suggests that it is all in fun.

Along with the ability to tease adults comes an awareness of the meaning of "no." At ten months old, "no" to your baby meant stop for a second and then go ahead. Now, at twelve months old, "no" really stands for a prohibition. When an adult says "no" to a twelve month old child a common reaction is a show of temper, or a shower of tears.

Your baby's readiness to try out new things extends to the social realm. She is delighted with the opportunity to play with other children. With older children, especially siblings, your baby will watch for a while to see what toys the children are playing with. She will then devote all her efforts to getting her hands on those toys.

When the year old baby plays with a same age peer, the play is likely to progress from watching to modeling each other's actions. When peers know each other well, we may see a child offer a toy to her friend, or monitor her friend's expression when she takes a toy away. This kind of interactive play is a definite advance over nine month old peer interaction where a peer was likely to be treated as an interesting object to be pinched, poked and pulled at. Unquestionably, your baby recognizes the responsive qualities of a peer. During the next year, beginning with momentary exchanges and progressing to hour long intervals, she will learn the joy of playing with another child.

Playfulness, curiosity, a readiness to experiment, these are all the qualities that make your one year old a delightful companion. As you and your baby play together during the second year, you will become more and more aware of the ways in which she is developing as a unique and separate person. At times she will tease and defy you. At times she will use you as a resource. At times she will proudly share her new discoveries, and at times she will come to you for comfort and affection.

The second year of life will provide you and your baby with new challenges, new problems, and new opportunities to learn and grow. The time you spent with your baby during the first year, the games that you have played, and the love you have shared have prepared you to meet the challenges and reap the benefits of your baby's second year.

Setting the Stage

Invite Exploration

The twelve month old baby is an active experimenter who needs time by herself to carry on her constant investigations. Make your baby's environment fun to explore. Place cartons with interesting things inside them around the room. Hide a toy behind a chair, or tie ribbons on to toys that your baby can pull.

Share Your Baby's Discoveries

When baby finds something that seems to capture her interest: a shadow on the wall, a piece of foil that makes a crinkling sound, a smooth warm stone, talk about it with her. The more enthusiasm you show about the baby's discoveries, the more she is encouraged to explore and investigate.

Playtime

Making Discoveries:

Rainbow Walk

Suspend a six foot strip of corrugated cardboard between a door frame. Tape each end at the bottom of the door. The cardboard will make an arch—rainbow. Baby will learn about spatial relationships as she attempts to crawl under, walk under, back under, or ride her riding toys under the rainbow. She will learn how tall she is as well as how wide she is.

Sift

A soup strainer is a good toy for the sandbox. It is easy for baby to manipulate, and she will experiment with holding it at different heights as she watches the sand pour out.

Make a Cardboard Hill

Fold a piece of cardboard to make a hill. Show the baby how to place the car on top of the hill and let it roll down.

Junk Toy

Stringing odd rattles, toys and containers on a cord makes a silly wonderful pull toy. Soon baby will bring you things to add to her toy.

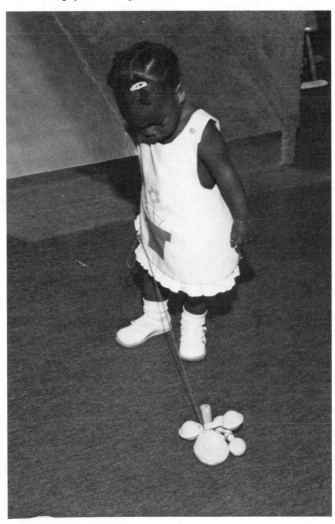

Explorations

Play hide and seek with baby's toys. The more you play naming games with your baby, the more opportunities she has to learn language.

Older Friends

If your baby doesn't have siblings, invite some preschool children over to play. Your baby will attempt to mimic what they are doing and you will be surprised at how many new things she learns.

Stacking Blocks

Large cardboard nesting alphabet blocks make a wonderful first birthday present. They can be used in a variety of ways, as containers, as building blocks, and as a nesting toy.

Let Baby Scribble

The high chair is an ideal spot to practice scribbling. Because your baby is more interested in manipulating the crayon than producing a work of art, let her practice on scrap paper or a newspaper.

Playing Parent

Give your baby a stroller or shopping cart and send her for a stroll with her doll. Pretending and language development go together.

Improving Coordination:

Play a Raking Game

Make the baby a rake out of a stick and a comb. Sit her at a table and show her how to use the rake to gather out-of-reach toys. Make sure that you play this game only while the baby is sitting down. Letting the baby walk around with a stick is not a good idea.

Play Shadows

Take the baby out on a sunny day and show her shadows. Stand on her shadow and let the baby stand on yours.

Throw a Bean Bag

Give her a bean bag and a large pail. Show her how to throw the bean bag into the pail.

Ball Play

Roll a beach ball or large plastic ball down a slight incline, or toss it against the wall and let the baby chase it. This will help her develop motor control.

Stepping High

If your baby is walking now, put a row of blocks in front of her and let her step over it. This will give her practice in maintaining her balance.

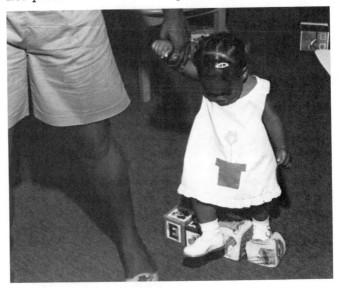

Make a Tunnel

Make a tunnel by spreading your legs and let your baby walk through. This will help her learn more about position in space.

Tie a Ribbon

If your baby is walking, tie a ribbon on to a stuffed animal and send her off on a pet walk.

Sit-On Toy

If your baby is walking steadily she is probably ready for a sit-on push toy. Make sure that the one you buy is stable and is low enough for your baby to get on by herself.

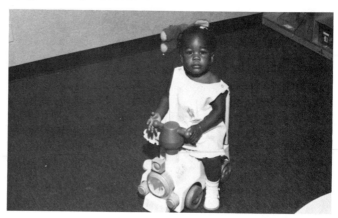

Clothespin Game

Show your baby how to slip old fashion clothespins around the rim of a coffee can. This is a great game for developing eye-hand coordination.

Mommy's Helper

Give your baby a sponge so that she can help wipe her own highchair.

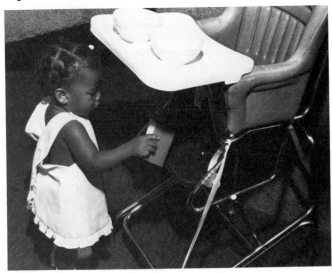

Mini Chair

Babies who have learned to walk enjoy the challenge of sitting by themselves in a small chair. Look for a sturdy canvas or cushioned chair that is wide enough for your baby to climb in frontwards and then turn around. In the beginning babies have difficulty backing into chairs.

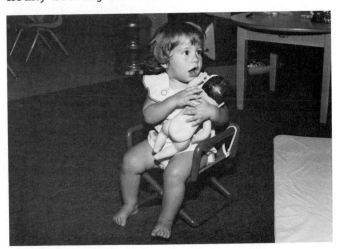

Hammer Toy

Now that your baby has developed good eye hand coordination, she will enjoy practicing her banging skills on a responsive target. Many hammer toys are available with figures that pop up when banged on.

Solving Problems:

Shoe Find

Rainy days often stretch Mother's imagination. Place one pair of shoes in a pile. Remove one and give it to your baby. Tell her to get the other side. If she succeeds in finding the "match" add another pair of shoes. If your baby has difficulty, show her the shoe that matches.

Purse Play

Give your baby an old wallet, some keys and a purse. Your baby will feel important carrying around these "grown up" possessions. At the same time your baby will attempt to open the purse, place the wallet inside the purse, or place the key in a keyhold. She is making important real world connections.

Blocks

Build a block tower out of alphabet blocks. Give your child a turn.

Magic Cups

Your baby's thinking ability cannot be stressed enough. She will enjoy activities that provide a challenge. Place two cups in front of baby. Place a small toy under one cup. Ask baby, "Where is the toy?" Lift the cup to show her where it is. Do this several times. Then let the baby lift the correct cup.

Color Spools

Give your baby a container with a lid, several regular size spools painted blue, and one giant size spool painted red. Make a hole in the lid big enough for the regular size blue spool but too small for the red spool. Your baby will discover which spools fit in the hole.

Push Car

Give your baby a toy car. See if she can push it along the floor. Tie a string to the car. Now is she able to pull it?

Push Car Through Tunnel

Make a tunnel out of a cereal box. Show your baby how to push a car through the tunnel. Your baby will watch for her car at the other end.

Tube Play

Give your baby a long cardboard tube from the center of a gift wrapping roll. Show her how the tube can be used to push a ball along the floor.

Bathe the Baby Doll

Put a large baby doll in the bath with your baby. Wash the baby doll's hair. Now let your baby have a turn.

Quiet Time:

Cups and Saucers

Before your baby masters the art of counting, she must understand the concept of one. You can use unbreakable cups and saucers as tools. Place a saucer in front of your baby. Instruct her to place a cup on the saucer. Add more cups and more saucers, talking about "one more saucer" and "one more cup."

Pop-Up Man

Thread a straw through a paper cup. Attach a piece of round cardboard to the top. Decorate it or make it look like a face using scraps of fabric and yarn. Show your baby how to pull the straw and make the face disappear into the cup, then push up the straw and make the face reappear.

Make Baby a Family Album

Make your baby her own family album. Be sure to include your baby's favorite people and favorite pets.

Read to Baby

Read to your baby. See if she is ready to turn the pages by herself.

Make a First Birthday Scrap Book

Save cards, invitations and ribbons from your baby's first party and put them in an album along with a sequence of birthday party photos. Baby will continue to enjoy her first birthday party as you read the album together.

A Closing Thought

You are your baby's first teacher—but in a manner of speaking, your baby is your teacher, too. Every baby that comes into this world is a unique personality making an indelible impression on the people who care for him, enriching their lives in a thousand subtle ways. As you watch your baby grow and learn in these early months of life, you, his parents, share in the learning experience.

This book includes a variety of games and activities. Be selective—choose the activities that seem right for you and your baby. If he tends to be inactive, you might want to choose games that encourage movement. If he does not pay attention to sounds, you might want to choose games that involve listening. Most important, make sure that you and your baby have fun with the activities you select. Only through a succession of happy experiences can your baby develop the confidence in himself that will allow him to explore and investigate his world.

Perhaps you have noticed that some of the suggested activities are repeated in different months. This kind of repetition is important for infants. An old experience "revisited" can provide a new opportunity to learn as the baby brings new capabilities into the learning situation.

Remember, too, that even at a very young age your baby will enjoy the company of another baby. Invite some friends over with their baby. As you try out the activities together, you will double the fun of "baby watching."

SUGGESTED READINGS:

Brazelton, T. B. *Infants and Mothers*, New York: Dell Publishing, 1969.

Brazelton, T. B. *On Becoming a Family*, New York: Delacorte Press/Seymour Lawrence, 1981.

Burck, F. W. *Baby Sense, A Practical and Supportive Guide to Baby Care*, New York: St. Martin's Press, 1979.

Caldwell, B. "The Effects of Infant Care," *Review of Child Development Research, I* (New York: Russell Sage Foundation), 1964.

Editors of Consumers Reports. *Consumers Union Guide to Buying for Babies*, New York: Warner Books, 1975.

Costanzo, C. *Mommy and Me Exercises, The Kidnastics Program*, California: Cougar Books, 1983.

Early Learning Corp. "The Growing Child," Indiana: Dunn & Hargitt, Inc.

Fraiberg, S. *The Magic Years*, New York: Scribners, 1959.

Free Stuff Editors. *Free Stuff for Kids*, revised ed., Minnesota: Meadowbrook Press, 1980.

Green, M. *A Sigh of Relief: The First-Aid Handbook for Childhood Emergencies*, New York: Bantam Books, 1977.

Heinl, T. *The Baby Massage Book: Using Touch for Better Bonding and Happier Babies*, New Jersey: Prentice-Hall, Inc., 1983.

Johnson & Johnson Baby Products Company. *The First Wonderous Year: You and Your Baby*, New York: Macmillan, 1979.

Jones, S. *Crying Baby, Sleepless Nights*, New York: Warner Books, 1983.

Jones, S. *Good Things for Babies*, Boston: Houghton Mifflin, 1980.

Karnes, M. *You and Your Small Wonder: Activities for Busy Parents and Babies*, Ohio: American Guidance, 1982.

Kelly, M. and Parsons, E. *The Mother's Almanac*, New York: Doubleday & Co., 1975.

Leach, P. *Your Baby and Child: From Birth to Age Five*, New York: Alfred Knopf, 1978.

Levy J. *The Baby Exercise Book: The First Fifteen Months*, New York: Pantheon Books, 1974.

McBride, A. *The Growth and Development of Mothers*, New York: Harper & Row, 1981.

Nance, S. *Premature Babies: A Handbook for Parents*, New York: Arbor House, 1982.

Painter, G. *Teach Your Baby*, New York: Simon & Schuster, 1971.

Schneider, V. *Infant Massage, A Handbook for Loving Parents*, New York: Bantam Books, 1982.

Sills, B. and Henry, J. *Mother to Mother Baby Care*, New York: Avon Books, 1981.

Tronick, E. and Adamson, L. *Babies as People: New Findings on Social Beginnings*, New York: Collier Books/Collier Macmillan Publishers, 1980.

White, B. *The First Three Years of Life*, New Jersey: Prentice-Hall, Inc., 1975.

Suggested Books for Babies:

Bonforte, L., illus. *Farm Animals*, New York: Random House, 1981.

Brown, M. *Good Night Moon*, New York: Harper & Row, 1947, 1977.

Durrel, J., illus. *The Pudgy Book of Toys*, New York: Putnam Publishing Group, 1983.

Hill, E. *At Home*, New York: Random House, 1983.

Hill, E. *My Pets*, New York: Random House, 1983.

Hill, E. *The Park*, New York: Random House, 1983.

Hill, E. *Spot's Birthday Party*, New York: Putnam Publishing Group, 1982.

Hill, E. *Spot's First Walk*, New York: Putnam Publishing Group, 1981.

Hill, E. *Up There*, New York: Random House, 1983.

Johnson, A., illus. *Soft as a Kitten*, New York: Random House, 1982.

Kahn, P. *Did You Ever Pet a Care Bear?*, New York: Random House, 1983.

Kunhardt, D. *Pat the Bunny*, New York: Golden Press/Western Publishing, 1962.

McNaught, H. *Baby Animals*, New York: Random House, 1976.

Object Lesson Series. *A First Book In My Garden*, England: Brimax Books, 1980.

Object Lesson Series. *A First Book In My Nursery*, England: Brimax Books, 1980.

Object Lesson Series. *A First Book In My Toy Box*, England: Brimax Books, 1980.

Wells, R. *Max's First Word*, New York: Dial Books for Young Readers, 1979.

Wilburn, K., illus. *Pudgy Pals*, New York: Putnam Publishing Group, 1983.

Witte, E. and Witte, P. *The Touch Me Book*, New York: Golden Press/Western Publishing, 1961.

Keeping Up With Baby . . .

It's fun to keep track of what your baby does. On these pages list some of the things you notice about your baby—what he or she looks like, favorite toys and activities, new accomplishments, family events.

Keeping Up With Baby . . .

Keeping Up With Baby . . .

Keeping Up With Baby . . .

Keeping Up With Baby . . .

Keeping Up With Baby . . .

The first few years of your baby's life are very important. It's the time when he or she is learning to walk, talk, recognize people and many other things.

Some babies may have trouble developing certain skills. Parents are often the first to notice when their child is not learning or growing like other infants they know.

If you have any concerns about your baby, there is someone who can answer your questions. You can call First Steps at **1-800-234-1448**. Remember too, it's important for all infants to have "well baby" check ups by their doctor every three months for the first year and a half, and at least every six months after that until they're three years old.

About the Author

Marilyn Segal, Ph.D., a developmental psychologist specializing in early childhood, is professor of human development and director of the Family Center at Nova University in Fort Lauderdale, Florida. The mother of five children, she is the author of sixteen books, including *Making Friends, Just Pretending,* and the four-volume series *Your Child at Play.* She is also the creator of the nine-part television series "To Reach a Child."

Parenting and Child Care Books Available from Newmarket Press

Lynda Madaras Talks to Teens About AIDS
An Essential Guide for Parents, Teachers, and Young People
by Lynda Madaras

Written especially for parents, teachers, and young adults aged 14 through 19, this valuable book describes with honesty and sensitivity what AIDS is, why teens need to know about it, how it is transmitted, and how to stay informed about it. Includes drawings, bibliography, resource guide. (96 pages, 5½ × 8¼, $14.95 hardcover, $5.95 paperback)

Lynda Madaras' Growing Up Guide for Girls
by Lynda Madaras with Area Madaras

For pre-teens and teens; an all-new companion workbook/journal to the *What's Happening to My Body? Book for Girls* to help girls further explore their changing bodies and their relationships with parents and friends; complete with quizzes, exercises, and space to record personal experiences. Includes drawings, photographs, bibliography. (256 pages, 7¼ × 9, $16.95 hardcover, $9.95 paperback)

The "What's Happening to My Body?" Book for Boys
A Growing Up Guide for Parents and Sons NEW EDITION
by Lynda Madaras, with Dane Saavedra

Written with candor, humor, and clarity, here is the much-needed information on the special problems boys face during puberty, and includes chapters on: changing size and shape; hair, perspiration, pimples, and voice changes; the reproductive organs; sexuality; and much more. "Down-to-earth, conversational treatment of a topic that remains taboo in many families"—*Washington Post*. Includes 34 drawings, charts, and diagrams, bibliography, index. (272 pages, 5½ × 8¼, $16.95 hardcover, $9.95, paperback)

The "What's Happening to My Body?" Book for Girls
A Growing Up Guide for Parents and Daughters NEW EDITION
by Lynda Madaras, with Area Madaras

Selected as a "Best Book for Young Adults" by the American Library Association, this carefully researched book provides detailed explanations of what takes place in a girl's body as she grows up. Includes chapters on: changing size and shape; changes in the reproductive organs; menstruation; puberty in boys; and much more. Includes 44 drawings, charts and diagrams, bibliography, index. (288 pages, 5½ × 8¼, $16.95 hardcover, $9.95 paperback)

The "What's Happening in My Life?" Workbook for Girls
by Lynda Madaras, with Area Madaras

The companion volume to the *"What's Happening to My Body?" Book for Girls*, this workbook/diary is filled with factual information, quizzes, and checklists, offering adolescent girls ages 9 to 15 an ideal opportunity to explore and set down in writing their feelings about the changes they are going through. Includes quizzes, checklists, exercises, illustrations and bibliography. (128 pages, 5½ × 8¼; $9.95 paperback)

How Do We Tell the Children?
Helping Children Understand and Cope When Someone Dies
by Dan Schaefer and Christine Lyons; foreword by David Peretz, M.D.

This valuable, commonsense book provides the straightforward language to help parents explain death to children from three-year-olds to teenagers, while including insights from numerous psychologists, educators, and clergy. Special features include a 16-page crisis-intervention guide to deal with situations such as accidents, AIDS, terminal illness, and suicide. "Parents need this clear, extremely readable guide . . . highly recommended"—*Library Journal.* (160 pages, 5½ × 8¼, $16.95 hardcover, $8.95 paperback)

Your Child At Play: Birth to One Year
Discovering the Senses and Learning About the World
by Marilyn Segal, Ph.D.

Focuses on the subtle developmental changes that take place in each of the first twelve months of life and features over 400 activities that parent and child can enjoy together during day-to-day routines. "Insightful, warm, and practical ... expert knowledge that's a must for every parent" (T. Berry Brazelton, M.D., Boston Children's Hospital). Includes over 250 photos, bibliography. (288 pages, 7¼ × 9, $21.95 hardcover, $10.95 paperback)

Your Child at Play: One to Two Years
Exploring, Daily Living, Learning, and Making Friends
by Marilyn Segal, Ph.D., and Don Adcock, Ph.D.

Contains hundreds of suggestions for creative play and for coping with everyday life with a toddler, including situations such as going out in public, toilet training, and sibling rivalry. "An excellent guide to the hows, whys, and what-to-dos of play . . . the toy and activity suggestions are creative and interesting"—*Publishers Weekly.* Includes over 300 photos, bibliography, index. (224 pages, 7¼ × 9, $16.95 hardcover, $9.95 paperback)

Your Child at Play: Two to Three Years
Growing Up, Language, and the Imagination
by Marilyn Segal, Ph.D., and Don Adcock, Ph.D.

Provides vivid descriptions of how two-year-olds see themselves, learn language, learn to play imaginatively, get along with others and make friends, and explore what's around them, and uses specific situations to describe and advise on routine problems and concerns common to this age, especially that of self-definition. Includes over 175 photos, bibliography, index. (208 pages, 7¼ × 9, $16.95 hardcover, $9.95 paperback)

Your Child at Play: Three to Five Years
Conversation, Creativity, and Learning Letters, Words, and Numbers
by Marilyn Segal, Ph.D., and Don Adcock, Ph.D.

Hundreds of practical, innovative ideas for encouraging and enjoying the world of the preschooler, with separate sections devoted to conversational play, discovery play, creative play, playing with letters and numbers, and playing with friends. Includes 100 photos, bibliography, index. (224 pages, 7¼ × 9, $16.95 hardcover, $9.95 paperback)

"Your Child at Play" Starter Set
Three paperback volumes, covering birth through three years, in a colorful shrink-wrapped boxed set. The perfect gift for parents, teachers, and care-givers. ($29.85)

How to Shoot Your Kids on Home Video
Moviemaking for the Whole Family
by David Hajdu

The perfect book for the video-age family and classroom—from the former editor of *Video Review*. Offers parents and teachers a lively, "user-friendly" look at making wonderful home-movie videos, featuring 11 ready-to-shoot scripts. Includes photos, index. (208 pages, 7¼ × 9, $10.95 paperback)

Baby Massage
Parent-Child Bonding Through Touching
by Amelia D. Auckett; Introduction by Dr. Tiffany Field.

A fully illustrated, practical, time-tested approach to the ancient art of baby mas-sage. Topics include: bonding and body contact; baby massage as an alternative to drugs; healing the effects of birth trauma; baby massage as an expression of love; and more. "For anyone concerned with the care and nurturing of infants"—*Bookmarks*. Includes 34 photos and drawings, bibliography, index. (128 pages, 5½ × 8¼, $9.95 paperback)

In Time and With Love
Caring for the Special Needs Baby
by Marilyn Segal, Ph.D.

From a psychologist and mother of a handicapped daughter, sensitive, practical advice on play and care for children who are physically handicapped, developmentally delayed, or constitutionally difficult. Topics include: developing motor skills, learning language, and developing problem-solving abilities; interacting with siblings, family members and friends; handling tough decision-making; and much more. Includes 50 photos, six resource guides, bibliography, and index. (208 pages, 7¼ × 9, $21.95 hardcover, $12.95 paperback)

Raising Your Jewish/Christian Child
How Interfaith Parents Can Give Children the Best of Both Their Heritages
by Lee F. Gruzen

Based on hundreds of interviews as well as the author's extensive research and personal experience, this pioneering guide details how people have worked out their own paths in Jewish/Christian marriages, and how they have given their children and themselves a solid foundation to seek their own identity. Includes new forewords by Rabbi Lavey Derby and the Reverend Canon Joel A. Gibson, bibliography, and index. (288 pages, 5 5/16 × 8, $10.95 paperback)

Saying No Is Not Enough
Raising Children Who Make Wise Decisions About Drugs and Alcohol
by Robert Schwebel, Ph.D.
Introduction by Benjamin Spock, M.D.

Widely praised as the first book to present a complete program on how to empower children to defend themselves against drugs, this easy-to-read, step-by-step guide shows parents and counselors how to help kids build the self-confidence and develop the life skills necessary to make life-protecting decisions about drugs and alcohol. "Wise and wondrously specific: a solid parental manual."—*Kirkus Reviews*. Includes bibliography, index. (256 pages, 5 5/16 × 8, $18.95 hardcover, $9.95 paperback)

Please see next page for order form.

Ask for these titles at your local bookstore or

Use this coupon or write to: NEWMARKET PRESS,
18 East 48th Street, NY, NY 10017.

Please send me:

Auckett, BABY MASSAGE
___$9.95 paperback (1-55704-022-2)

Gruzen, RAISING YOUR
JEWISH/CHRISTIAN CHILD
___$10.95 paperback (1-55704-059-1)

Hajdu, HOW TO SHOOT YOUR KIDS
ON HOME VIDEO
___ $10.95 paperback (1-55704-013-3)

Madaras, LYNDA MADARAS'
GROWING UP GUIDE FOR GIRLS
___ $16.95 hardcover (0-937858-87-0)
___ $9.95 paperback (0-937858-74-9)

Madaras, LYNDA MADARAS TALKS
TO TEENS ABOUT AIDS
___ $14.95 hardcover (1-55704-010-9)
___ $5.95 paperback (1-55704-009-5)

Madaras, "WHAT'S HAPPENING TO
MY BODY?" BOOK FOR BOYS
___ $16.95 hardcover (1-55704-002-8)
___ $9.95 paperback (0-937858-99-4)

Madaras, "WHAT'S HAPPENING TO
MY BODY?" BOOK FOR GIRLS
___ $16.95 hardcover (1-55704-001-X)
___ $9.95 paperback (0-937858-98-6)

Madaras, "WHAT'S HAPPENING
IN MY LIFE?" WORKBOOK FOR
GIRLS
___$9.95 paperback (1-55704-080-X)

Schaefer/Lyons, HOW DO WE TELL
THE CHILDREN?
___ $16.95 hardcover (0-937858-60-9)
___ $8.95 paperback (1-55704-015-X)

Schwebel, SAYING NO IS NOT
ENOUGH
___$18.95 hardcover (1-55704-041-9)
___$9.95 paperback (1-55704-078-8)

Segal, IN TIME AND WITH LOVE
___ $21.95 hardcover (0-937858-95-1)
___ $12.95 paperback (0-937858-96-X)

Segal, YOUR CHILD AT PLAY: BIRTH
TO ONE YEAR
___ $21.95 hardcover (0-937858-50-1)
___ $10.95 paperback (0-937858-51-X)

Segal/Adcock, YOUR CHILD AT
PLAY: ONE TO TWO YEARS
___ $16.95 hardcover (0-937858-52-8)
___ $9.95 paperback (0-937858-53-6)

Segal/Adcock, YOUR CHILD AT
PLAY: TWO TO THREE YEARS
___ $16.95 hardcover (0-937858-54-4)
___ $9.95 paperback (0-937858-55-2)

Segal/Adcock, YOUR CHILD AT
PLAY: THREE TO FIVE YEARS
___ $16.95 hardcover (0-937858-72-2)
___ $9.95 paperback (0-937858-73-0)

Segal/Adcock, "YOUR CHILD AT
PLAY" STARTER SET (Vols. 1, 2, & 3
in paperback gift box set)
___ $29.85 (0-937858-77-3)

For postage and handling add $2.00 for the first book, plus $1.00 for each
additional book. Allow 4-6 weeks for delivery. Prices subject to change.
I enclose check or money order payable to NEWMARKET PRESS in the amount
of $_____.

NAME _____

ADDRESS _____

CITY/STATE/ZIP _____

For quotes on quantity purchases, or for a copy of our catalog, please write or
phone Newmarket Press, 18 East 48th Street, NY, NY 10017. 1-212-832-3575.